Praise for

Invisible Solutions

"Stephen Shapiro is an engineer who can communicate in clear, plain language. And in this smart and practical book, he uses his considerable skills to help you fashion fresh solutions to your toughest challenges. By enlisting Shapiro's 25 lenses, you'll see your business problems more clearly—and come up with creative answers that will boggle your mind and delight your customers."

Daniel H. Pink, author of *When*, *Drive*, and *To Sell Is Human*

"*Invisible Solutions* is an essential read for anyone faced with seemingly intractable business issues or simply looking for non-traditional approaches to traditional problem-solving. Stephen Shapiro's extensive consulting background serves him well, offering practical insights and approaches that can be immediately applied to any industry. This is an exceptional tool to help uncover solutions that might well otherwise remain unexplored, untapped, and hidden."

Adam Burke, Chief Operating Officer, Los Angeles Tourism and Convention Board

"Stephen Shapiro has captured the essence of what I believe: Innovation is not about novelty or ideas—it is about defining and solving important problems. And using 25 lenses, he shows the innovation community how they can solve these important problems using commonsense solutions hidden in plain sight!"

Navin Kunde, innovation leader, The Clorox Company

"This book is a gift for leaders and innovation professionals everywhere! With *Invisible Solutions*, you will stop solving problems that don't matter and start getting the results you want and need."

Jack Elkins, founder, Sidekick Innovation, and former Director of Innovation, NBA's Orlando Magic

"Sometimes the best solutions are right in front of your nose. This book will help you see solutions that you may have missed."

Matthew Von Ertfelda, Senior Vice President, Global Operations (Food and Beverage), Marriott International

"Finally, an innovation book that can be used by everyone, every day. This is actually more than a book—it is a powerful tool that transforms complex problems into simple (and practical) solutions. If you are looking to take your organization to the next level, the solution is *Invisible Solutions!*"

Dorie Clark, author of *Entrepreneurial You* and *Reinventing You*, and executive education faculty, Duke University Fuqua School of Business

"The first and most important step in any innovation process is shifting your lens to make hidden opportunities visible. Stephen Shapiro gets below the buzzwords to provide us with 25 new and practical innovation lenses to help us identify and commercialize new breakthrough solutions. *Invisible Solutions* is a must-read for any leader working hard to stay relevant in these rapidly changing times."

Saul Kaplan, founder and Chief Catalyst, Business Innovation Factory (BIF)

"*Invisible Solutions* is truly transformational. Stephen Shapiro cuts through preconceptions about problem solving and innovation like a neurosurgeon—severing presuppositions and making surprising, useful, and unexpected new connections. This book is inspiring, insightful, and filled with practical tools to help you apply what you learn. Read this book. Share it with your team. It will positively change how you think, what you do, and the results you get."

Karl J. Newman, Chairman, President and CEO, WSRB/Building Metrix, Inc.

"In this insightful and refreshing book, Stephen has taken me to a different level of thinking. *Invisible Solutions* provides practical advice on how to focus on what matters most. The book is like a lighthouse of innovation and has positively impacted my daily work and personal life."

Ping Zhong, Vice President, Human Nutrition Science and Technology, Archer Daniels Midland

"If you're looking for breakthrough tools for innovation, this is just what you need! Approaching innovation with a clearly defined challenge statement accelerates progress in discovering a powerful solution. We used the lenses from the book in a recent leadership workshop and had several breakthroughs in thinking that would not have happened without this powerful tool. This is a must-read book!"

Thonda Boals Barnes, St. Jude Leadership Academy, St. Jude Children's Research Hospital

"In business leadership we look at problems as opportunities for us to solve. We like to think we gather the data, understand the facts and feelings, get to the root problem, and build sound action plans to solve such problems. However, through the work and writings of Stephen Shapiro, you have to ask yourself, *Are you asking the right questions?* His knowledge and delivery remind us at CertaPro Painters, Ltd. that oftentimes we look at all of our issues through the wrong lens. When you change your perspective, you are better positioned to ask better questions and thus change the paradigm leading to solving better problems, but doing it faster and in ways never thought possible."

Michael Stone, President and CEO, CertaPro Painters, Ltd.

"Culture drives success more than any strategy, and Stephen Shapiro is the ultimate expert on creating a culture of innovation. Reading just one chapter of *Invisible Solutions* will help you maximize returns on any project. Read the entire book and you will have the tools to transform your entire organization."

Robert Richman, former Culture Strategist, Zappos Insights, and author of *The Culture Blueprint*

"Asking great questions is the foundation for successful leadership. Whether you are connecting with your team or solving problems with/for them, it all starts with your ability to ask the right questions. *Invisible Solutions* is an incredibly powerful book that equips you with the tools to ask effective questions to solve any problem you may encounter!"

Chris Goede, President, Corporate Leadership Solutions, The John Maxwell Company

"There have been so many times in the past where I have been searching for EXACTLY how to solve a business challenge. *Invisible Solutions* delivers the tools to help you rapidly find the answers you are looking for."

Phil M Jones, author of *Exactly What to Say*

"When you feel stuck, a good question can get you unstuck. But which question? Stephen Shapiro gives you the discipline to think differently by showing you the 25 lenses that can open up new possibilities, whether you're trying to solve an R&D challenge at work, or trying to make your home life a little happier."

Michael Bungay Stanier, *Wall Street Journal* bestselling author of *The Coaching Habit*

"Stephen's book offers a myriad of outside-the-box solutions for everyday problems that will make you a better leader or business owner. This book forces readers to look at business through different prisms, ask the right questions in order to change, challenge the status quo, and steamroll obstacles. Are you ready to push boundaries? Start reading this book now!"

Jeffrey Hayzlett, primetime TV and podcast host, speaker, author, and part-time cowboy

"*Invisible Solutions* is a must-read for anyone tackling complex and seemingly impossible business problems. Read this book and you will learn how to uncover amazing solutions you didn't know were possible."

Daniel Burrus, *New York Times* bestselling author of seven books including *Flash Foresight*

"*Invisible Solutions* is the book you've been waiting for—the one that points out your blind spots and enables you to make better decisions based on key lenses you've never even thought about before. You feel smarter, more empowered, and ready to innovate after reading this book!"

Traci Fenton, founder and CEO, WorldBlu

"*Invisible Solutions* provides a clear and pragmatic approach to reframing questions for innovative problem-solving."

Jeff Davis, founder and CEO, Exploring 4 Solutions

"Question everything! If you want to tell the story of innovation, and communicate the value of what is hard to explain, then *Invisible Solutions* is a book for you. Stephen Shapiro delivers the magic: how to give voice to the unseen with a rubric for better questions, dialogue, and breakthrough ideas. The 25 lenses are a unique, powerful guide to how humans think and make meaning. Read this book and go forth with better stories to tell."

Michael Margolis, CEO, Storied, and author of *Story 10x: Turn the Impossible Into the Inevitable*

"The old saying is that good things come in small packages, and in the case of *Invisible Solutions*, this is truer than ever. This small but powerful book shines a light on critical opportunities you can't afford to overlook."

Shep Hyken, customer service/experience expert, and *New York Times* bestselling author

"Incredibly useful and highly recommended! You'll turn to it again and again when confronted with almost any business problem."

Jay Baer, founder, Convince & Convert, and co-author of *Talk Triggers*

"In this smart, fast-moving book, Stephen Shapiro lays the foundation to help you solve complex business problems. Steve takes his 25 lenses, breaks them down into actionable 'do-this-now' steps, and gives you plenty of mind-sparking examples to chew on. If you're looking to upgrade your career, your team, and your results—look no further. The problem-solving book for the rest of us is here. Buy a copy for everyone on your team. Yes, it's that good."

David Newman, CSP, author of *Do It! Marketing* and *Do It! Speaking*

"It was a thrill to read Stephen Shapiro's latest book, *Invisible Solutions*. I've been a big fan of his thinking on innovation for over a decade. *Invisible Solutions* is his best (and smartest) book to date. When it comes to innovation, many companies think about speed and doing more of it. Stephen nails it: how about better? When you ask better questions, you get better solutions. When you can reframe the difficult problems, you wind up with something better. So, get better...read *Invisible Solutions* and watch how clarity and reframing creates immediate opportunities for your business to innovate."

Mitch Joel, author of *Six Pixels of Separation* and *Ctrl Alt Delete*

"Applying even one of Stephen Shapiro's 25 lenses for reframing problems will expand your mind, immediately shift your business, and help you see the world differently all at once. It quickly made me want to wait in lines longer at Disney, take my time in the airport, and liberally ponder the prevention of viscous shear in dense liquid! *Invisible Solutions* gives me the confidence to solve any business problem by seeing through lenses I didn't know were always right in front of me!"

Jason Hewlett, CSP, CPAE, Speaker Hall of Fame, and author of *The Promise to The One*

"Innovation is more than just coming up with creative ideas. It's about finding solutions to critical business challenges. *Invisible Solutions* provides practical insights and tools to help you solve your most difficult challenges and help drive growth and profits in a rapidly changing world."

Lt. Col. Waldo Waldman, author of the *New York Times* and *Wall Street Journal* bestseller *Never Fly Solo*

"The quality of your work is directly tied to the quality of your questions. *Invisible Solutions* will unlock brilliant ideas hiding in plain sight. A must-read for anyone who solves problems for a living."

Todd Henry, author of *Herding Tigers*

"Shapiro provides actionable wisdom to solve any difficult challenge in *Invisible Solutions*. He illustrates the mistakes of the wrong questions and guides you to the right ones. Most important, he delivers 25 lenses that allow you to see any obstacle from a new perspective to drive innovation, accelerate results, and enhance collaboration. Whether you are leading a sales organization, an entire division, or a team of colleagues, *Invisible Solutions* will help you see answers you didn't know were there."

Ian Altman, keynote speaker, business growth expert, and bestselling co-author of *Same Side Selling*

"Innovation at its core is about problem solving, but you need to make sure you're solving the right problem. This book teaches you how."

David Burkus, author of *The Myths of Creativity*

www.amplifypublishing.com

Invisible Solutions: 25 Lenses that Reframe and
Help Solve Difficult Business Problems

For more information, please contact:
Amplify Publishing, an imprint of Mascot Books
620 Herndon Parkway #320
Herndon, VA 20170
info@mascotbooks.com

www.InvisibleSolutionsBook.com
www.StephenShapiro.com

Library of Congress Control Number: 2019915921

CPSIA Code: PRFRE1219A
ISBN-13: 978-1-64543-186-2

Printed in Canada

There is no such thing as a new idea. It is impossible. We simply take a lot of old ideas and put them into a sort of mental kaleidoscope. We give them a turn and they make new and curious combinations. We keep on turning and making new combinations indefinitely; but they are the same old pieces of colored glass that have been in use through all the ages.

Mark Twain

INVISIBLE
SOLUTIONS

**25 Lenses that Reframe and
Help Solve Difficult Business Problems**

STEPHEN M. SHAPIRO

amplify
an imprint of Mascot Books

CONTENTS

CHAPTER 5
Reduce Abstraction

CHAPTER 6
Increase Abstraction

CHAPTER 7
Change Perspective

CHAPTER 8
Switch Elements

CHAPTER 9
Zero-In

SECTION 3
CHALLENGE-CENTERED INNOVATION

66

*The process for driving better results
doesn't start with great ideas—
it starts with better questions.*

A Left-Brained Approach to Innovation

Growing up, I was not cool. The more popular kids picked on me. In hindsight, I understand why. I loved chemistry, physics, and calculus. I was a member of the math club. Even my artistic endeavors, like marching band, were uncool. Let's face it: I was a nerd.

My love of all things geeky continued through college, where I majored in industrial engineering. I learned about statistics, probability, and computer simulations, and how all of that applies to manufacturing productivity.

The early part of my career with Accenture, a global management consulting firm, focused on these engineering-type activities. All of my work involved analysis, technical skills, and methodology. I spent my first years as a computer programmer. In the early 1990s, I got involved with process improvement work to make companies more efficient—"business process reengineering." This work was so geeky, it even had the word "engineering" in it.

I quickly learned that if companies optimize their processes, they will downsize their workforce. The tipping point came in 1995, when I was working on a project that resulted in ten thousand people losing their jobs.

I had an existential crisis.

It impacted me so deeply that I decided to take a six-month sabbatical to look back on my contributions to the world—both positive and negative. After several months of reflection, I had an epiphany: I wanted to shift gears. I no longer wanted to eliminate jobs; I wanted to create jobs. I decided to dedicate my business life to innovation, creativity, and helping companies grow.

But I found one problem: it was difficult being a left-brained engineer in this right-brained world. In the minds of many business leaders, innovation and creativity are artistic endeavors that involve free-thinking, lack of critical judgment, and little structure. But being a process guy at heart, I felt a little out of place. I craved structure.

Soon after I shifted my focus to innovation, I took part in a brainstorming session that felt like we were going nowhere, fast: lots of ideas, little value. The group mantra was "no idea is a bad idea." I did not share that opinion.

My engineering soul craved a more predictable approach. I didn't want to stifle the creative process, but I did want to make it more efficient, like I had with other business processes.

So, I reverse-engineered the results companies wanted, and I quickly discovered that the best way to get there was, indeed, an engineering-style approach. The process for driving better results doesn't start with great ideas—it starts with better questions.

When I tested this approach with others, I saw that innovation was not just the domain of the naturally creative. Anyone can contribute, even nerds like me. Everyone is creative and innovative, just in different ways.

Having been in the innovation space for more than twenty years now, I've seen a lot of changes. When I first started, innovation wasn't a word often used in companies; when it was, it was only for research and development groups that created physical products. Now, the word innovation is used everywhere. We have innovative $7,000 toilets with built-in Alexa voice controls, innovative cat litter boxes that send the owner a text message any time their feline poops, and a published list of innovative lawyers. The term is often used to describe anything that is unusual or novel, even if it is not valuable. It is one of the most overused, abused, and misunderstood words in business today.

It has become so pervasive and hyped that organizational antibodies want to fight it. Managers are tired of the term. Employees have no idea how to innovate (or what is expected of them). And leaders are disappointed with the results they've been getting. Besides, most people are busy worrying about today's results and this quarter's earnings—investing in the future with innovation feels like a distraction. Companies need to innovate to survive, but there never seems to be enough time.

Fortunately, when you apply the engineering approaches I've honed over the years with world-class organizations, you'll get amazing results with less effort, fewer resources, and reduced risk. The key is to recognize that innovation is not about novelty or ideas; it is about defining and solving important problems.

In the past, innovation seemed to be under the exclusive purview of creative people wearing long white robes and sitting on high mountains, who handed down the gospel for the future. However, when you view innovation through the perspective of problem-solving, you will discover that everyone can participate. It's not the domain of a few privileged individuals. It's not separate from the business—it *is* the business.

Problem-solving affects every part of an organization—sales, leadership, recruiting, marketing. Any part of the business that has problems and opportunities can leverage the techniques shared in this book.

Innovation and problem-solving are no longer solely about future investments. Everyone can solve challenges to produce results today.

A Better Approach to Better Solutions

The quality of your business and life are largely dependent on the quality of the problems you solve and the decisions you make. Problem-solving is one of the most important skills every individual, entrepreneur, employee, and leader needs. Without it, you cannot design your own path. You are limited to a default path that is an extrapolation of your past. The strategies and tactics you use to improve your business will be heavily influenced by what you have tried before, resulting in incremental change at best. In a world that changes at hyperspeed, incremental improvements ultimately make you irrelevant. Although we can't see them, the most valuable and practical solutions are often right under our noses. When done correctly, problem-solving can help us uncover those hidden opportunities.

> The quality of your business and life are largely dependent on the quality of the problems you solve and the decisions you make.

Large corporations face an endless sea of challenges:

- How can we avoid becoming a commodity?
- How can we increase revenues?
- How can we decrease costs?
- How can we make sure we are not disrupted by new technologies?

Small business owners, entrepreneurs, and solopreneurs also face a long list of challenges:

- How can we maintain better work–life balance?
- How can we deal with larger competitors that have more money and resources?
- How can we meet payroll each month?
- How can we differentiate our business?

Even life hands us personal challenges:

- How can we feed our families after losing our jobs?
- How can we find new jobs?
- How can we choose where to live?
- How can we get promoted at work?

When faced with these and myriad other challenges, we crave answers. It's a natural human instinct. But having answers is not *the* answer. Asking different and better questions is the key to finding better solutions. As you will see, the questions we ask affect the range of solutions we consider. Unfortunately, past experiences often influence the questions we ask. This can limit the potential of your business. If you are asking the wrong question, no matter how much time, money, or energy you invest, you will never find the best answer.

Do you want a thriving business that can grow faster than the competition? Do you want to stay relevant in the minds of your customers? Do you want a more powerful life? If so, you need to master problem-solving. And the first step is to ask the right questions.

How to Read This Book

Although innovation has been my area of expertise for the past twenty-five years, this book focuses on problem definition, problem-solving, critical thinking, and decision-making. These concepts are critical components of innovation and applicable to all areas of business—and every aspect of life. While most of the examples in this book are focused on business, the concepts we'll explore can also easily and effectively help you solve challenges in your personal life.

I'm giving you an immensely valuable and highly practical tool: twenty-five lenses for problem formulation. That's twenty-five different ways to reframe any challenge you face. These lenses are designed to help you ask better questions that generate better solutions, ultimately leading to better results.

This book is divided into three sections:

- **Section 1.** Asking Better Questions: We'll explore why asking the right question is so important and why we are naturally wired to ask terrible ones.
- **Section 2.** Twenty-Five Lenses for Reframing Problems: This is the tool portion. I'll explain each of the lenses and guide you in when and how to use them.
- **Section 3.** Challenge-Centered Innovation: Leveraging well-framed questions in your organization can create an efficient innovation engine. I'll show you how you can improve your return on investment (ROI) by tenfold or more over traditional innovation methods when you focus on solving challenges.

This book is not intended to be read straight through, cover-to-cover, like a traditional business book. I suggest you read section 1 first in order to fully understand the power of asking better questions. After that, you have a couple of options:

1. If you are a business leader or part of an innovation team looking to improve ROI, you might want to skip section 2 and go straight to section 3. Then you can circle back to section 2 and learn more about the lenses.

2. If you want to get started reframing challenges now, read section 2, then start practicing with the lenses.

My primary goal in writing this book is to help you solve nearly any business problem you might have. Although there are countless other books on problem-solving, most only provide theory—not the necessary tools. And the tools that *are* provided typically focus on finding answers, rather than asking better questions. As you will discover, finding solutions to the wrong problem is irrelevant. By changing the questions, you can uncover answers that were previously hidden from sight. And the tool to help you reframe those questions—and shine a light on invisible solutions—are the twenty-five lenses.

ASKING BETTER QUESTIONS

66

The questions we ask have a profound impact on the range of solutions we can discover.

CHAPTER 1

Better Questions Lead to Better Answers

I travel nearly two hundred days a year, and like most road warriors, I am troubled by the fact that airlines restrict carry-on allotments to toaster-sized bags. It makes checked luggage the only option for trips longer than a day or two. After an exhausting day of travel, the last thing you want to do is wait at baggage claim for your luggage to (hopefully) arrive.

Unfortunately, we wait. In fact, a smaller U.S. airport surveyed their passengers and discovered that their biggest complaint was wait times at baggage claim. After some analysis, the airport determined that, on average, bags took fifteen to twenty minutes to get from the plane to the baggage carousel.

Being good innovators, they took to the task of "speeding up the bags." They made a sizable investment on faster conveyors, additional baggage handlers, and newer technology. They successfully reduced the baggage delivery time to an average of eight to ten minutes—a massive improvement. Problem solved, right?

Not so fast!

When passengers were surveyed soon thereafter, their biggest complaint remained "baggage claim wait time."

All innovators know that there is a point of diminishing returns on any investment. It took a lot of time, money, and effort to reduce the transport time to eight minutes; it would be prohibitively expensive to reduce it to seven, six, or five minutes. It looked like the travelers would just have to wait . . .

Except the airport had an epiphany.

It took eight to ten minutes for the bags to get from the plane to the baggage carousel. But it only took the passengers one to three minutes to get from the plane to baggage claim.

So, what do you think they did?

You guessed it: Instead of speeding up the bags, they *slowed down* the passengers. They literally reconfigured the airport so that it would take the passengers eight to ten minutes to get from the plane to the baggage carousel. As a result, when the passengers arrived at baggage claim, their luggage was waiting for them. This solution was also a money-making proposition, as people were now walking past more stores and restaurants.

When passengers were asked once again if they were happy with the wait times at baggage claim, they were ecstatic.

Although the airport finally stumbled upon a solution, massive amounts of resources were needlessly expended in the process of learning what so many other companies have yet to discover: To get the right answer, you must first ask the right question.

The airport was solving the problem of bag speed when, in fact, they needed to focus on reducing wait time. "Bag speed" and "wait time" sound like similar issues, but they are different: "Wait time" involves both the speed of the bags *and* the speed of the passengers.

If you spend all your time and resources trying to speed up bags, you will never think to slow down passengers. The way we formulate questions and frame issues can inadvertently put blinders on us, obscuring our view to the best solutions.

We can take this line of thinking a bit further. Instead of asking

"How can we reduce the wait time?" we can change it to "How can we improve the wait experience?" By changing just two words, we unlock a new, even larger range of opportunities.

I live in Orlando, a place where people pay hundreds of dollars a day to wait in lines. Disney World, Universal Studios, and other theme parks have mastered the wait-time problem. Although their first approach is often to reduce the wait with tools like Fast Pass and Express Pass, which allow you to jump to the front of the line, sometimes the wait can't be eliminated. As a result, leaders at these theme parks are always looking for ways to improve the experience.

> The way we formulate questions and frame issues can inadvertently put blinders on us, obscuring our view to the best solutions.

One example I love comes from Universal Studios' "Race Through New York Starring Jimmy Fallon." The ride designers put a lot of energy into the wait experience. There is no line. Instead, when you arrive, you walk into a mock version of Rockefeller Center, where you can wander around and view exhibits from past *Tonight Show* hosts, play video games, sit in comfy chairs, charge your phone, and watch live entertainment like barbershop quartets. A colleague of mine who was involved with the ride development told me that during the initial tests, the waiting room was so much fun that people weren't going on the ride. Universal Studios figured out a way to bring the wait experience to a whole new level.

Airports could learn from them.

The questions we ask have a profound impact on the range of solutions we can discover. Unfortunately, most companies and individuals are walking around blind, not taking the time to ask the right questions. Working with hundreds of organizations during the past thirty years, I've discovered that the least understood step of innovation and problem-solving is *problem definition*.

Ask the Right Questions the Right Way

Successfully solving problems requires more than just asking the right questions—we also need to ask them in the right way. In the corporate world, it is all too common for questions to be posed in overly broad and abstract ways, like the default questions associated with suggestion boxes:

- "What ideas do you have for improving the business?"
- "What new products should we create?"
- "How can we increase revenues?"
- "How can we improve productivity?"
- "What new technologies should we invest in?"

These questions are the business equivalents of trying to solve world hunger: too broad and ineffectual. Broad questions will almost certainly produce broad, irrelevant, or impractical solutions.

We saw this play out with the Deepwater Horizon oil rig explosion back in 2010, when concerned citizens and scientists were asked "How can we stop the flow of oil?" Although 123,000 suggested were received, none actually solved the problem. Overly abstract questions invite a large number of low-quality solutions.

Our pull toward this ambiguity is not surprising. For decades, we have been told to "think outside the box" as shorthand for innovation. But this doesn't work. The brain does not like abstraction. If you give people blank sheets of paper, they will struggle to develop new ideas. And the ideas they do conceive will be the typical, obvious ones.

Why is that? Well, to deal with information overload, the brain looks for ways to find order in chaos. It does that by mapping new experiences to past experiences using one of two different strategies. When information is closely related to something we've experienced in the past and can be easily categorized, the part of the brain responsible for recognizing abstract images is activated. When information feels like an outlier, an exception or a novelty, the part of the brain responsible for the retrieval of memories, the hippocampus, is used. This might sound like the opposite of what you'd expect, but when we don't understand something, we try hard to map it to anything we do understand from our past in order to make sense of it. Unfortunately, our past experiences may have nothing to do with the matter at hand.

Why does this matter? If we don't redirect the thought process, when faced with new and ambiguous information, we will most likely map it to memories or to past experiences that have little or nothing to do with the future. This limits our range of thought and can lead to incremental solutions that are insufficient to address the rapid changes and challenges we face. Even worse, it can lead to irrelevant or invalid decisions.

The brain works most effectively and efficiently within appropriate boundaries and constraints. Thinking too broadly actually reduces the quality and relevancy of solutions. When we give people a well-framed challenge, we enable them to process information more easily, we reduce cognitive overload, and we help shape the mapping that the individual does.

On the other hand, asking questions that are too specific results in ineffective thinking. Constricting boundaries too tightly can result in inappropriate solutions, much the same way that asking questions that are too broad can. When we frame issues too narrowly, they are either solutions masquerading as questions or questions that are so specific and narrowly defined that they limit the potential range of places where we will even consider looking for solutions.

A great example of this comes from another oil spill: the *Exxon Valdez* tanker crash in 1989. For nearly twenty years, cleanup crews in Alaska tried to remove the 10.8 million gallons of oil that spilled into the icy waters of Prince William Sound. The cleanup process was hampered because as the oil-water mixture was extracted from the sound, it seemed to freeze. Oil experts were unsuccessful in solving the problem "How can we prevent an oil–water mixture from freezing?" This question implied that the issue was related to oil, water, and temperature. This narrow definition limited the solutions they considered.

Finally, in 2007, the team at InnoCentive (a popular crowdsourcing platform) recognized that the real problem was not related to oil or freezing. It was, in fact, a common fluid-dynamics issue called "viscous shear." This is a phenomenon in which the molecules of dense liquids seize when moved quickly. When the oil-freezing challenge was reframed to "How can we prevent viscous shear in a dense liquid?" the problem was solved in six weeks. The solution was provided by someone who once worked in the construction industry. He recognized that wet, dense cement was prone to a similar clogging issue when poured through chutes. He figured that if vibrations could keep cement from hardening, then a similar concept could be adapted to keep the oil in the tanks from seizing. His solution worked, solving a two-decade-old problem, because the new question enabled him to reveal a previously invisible solution.

In the children's story *Goldilocks and the Three Bears*, Goldilocks goes into a house with three beds. One is too soft, one is too hard, and one is just right.

too big
Broad and Abstract

just right
Maximum Likelihood of Being Solved

too small
Overly Specific and Single Discipline

These two default mechanisms demonstrate the Goldilocks Principle. Broad and abstract thinking is too soft. Specific and narrow thinking is too hard. To reach the best solutions to our problems, we need to aim for "just right."

If something is too abstract, we need to deconstruct it and break it into smaller pieces. If something is too specific, we need to widen the scope. The Deepwater Horizon example illustrates how abstraction invites low-value solutions, whereas the *Exxon Valdez* demonstrates how to reframe an overly specific question to one that is "just right."

It is that perfectly crafted question, correctly balanced between concrete and abstract, that will reveal a range of new and different solutions. The reality is that you don't want to think outside the box—you want to find a better box, a well-framed challenge that helps propel the organization forward.

Unfortunately, asking better questions is not a natural act for most of us. Einstein reputedly said, "If I had an hour to save the world, I would spend fifty-nine minutes defining the problem and one minute finding solutions." The reality is that most people spend sixty minutes either solving problems that are unimportant and poorly defined or waiting for an epiphany.

We see this conundrum play out time and time again when misguided leaders tell their employees, "Don't bring me problems; bring me solutions." This is terrible advice. We don't need more low-value ideas; we need better, meatier, and more important problems that can be reframed. Only then should we look for solutions.

For decades, I've witnessed organizations fail miserably at problem-solving, often because they don't see what they need to see and so fail to define the right problems and ask the right questions. Their failure to effectively define problems leads to irrelevant solutions. We can't fix what we can't see. What we see is brought into focus (or distorted) by the lenses we wear. These lenses are the mental filters that stand between our business problems and our best thinking about how to solve them.

How do we identify the lenses we're wearing right now? How do we try on better lenses? How do we learn to create these perfect questions?

By examining the questions we're asking.

> What we see is brought into focus (or distorted) by the lenses we wear.

This book contains twenty-five problem-formulation lenses that will guide you and your organization through the process of asking better questions. Twenty-five heuristics—each with examples—that will accelerate finding solutions. According to Webster, heuristics "involve or serve as an aid to learning, discovery, or problem-solving by experimental and especially trial-and-error methods." Think of the lenses as a kaleidoscope that allows you to see what's in front of you in different lights and from different angles. Through these clearer lenses, you'll be able to see different, clearer, faster, better solutions.

A fortune cookie I once received said, "You always have the right answers. They just sometimes answer the wrong questions." So true: If you ask the wrong question, no matter how hard you try, you will never find the right answer. Regardless of your role, industry, or company size, this book will help you and your organization change your fortune, so that you always focus on questions that will improve efficiency, reduce risk, and drive sustainable long-term success.

Good to Gone

If you are a leader in a successful company, you might assume that these concepts do not apply to you. Interestingly, the more successful you are, the *more* valuable these concepts will actually be. What worked for your company in the past might be the wrong strategy in the long term.

Consider the retailer Sears. In the 1960s, the company accounted for 1 percent of the gross domestic product of the United States; one out of every two hundred workers in the United States received a paycheck from Sears. By 1972, two out of every three Americans shopped at Sears in any three-month period, and more than one out of every two households had a Sears credit card. They weren't just the world's largest retailer; they were a dominant force in the U.S. economy.

In 1983, Sears was more than ten times the size of Walmart. By October 1989, just six short years later, Walmart was the world's largest retailer, and Sears began a rapid decline.

Sears filed for bankruptcy in December 2018, emerging only after a $5.2 billion bid from former CEO Eddie Lampert. As of this writing, its future is uncertain. In the retail space, Sears is pretty much irrelevant. In the meantime, Amazon, Alibaba, and others are chipping away at even Walmart's dominance.

Sears' fall from grace is, of course, not unique. Pan American Airways, once the world's largest airline, became extinct in 1991. In the 1960s, the Howard Johnson's restaurant chain (remember those orange roofs?) was larger than Burger King, KFC, and McDonald's combined; today, only one HoJos remains. Although the book *Good to Great* featured Circuit City, it would have been more appropriate in the book *Good to Gone*, as the electronics retailer, too, is out of business.

The list of defunct former-greats continues to expand nearly every day. Toys "R" Us: Gone. Radio Shack: Gone. Lehman Brothers: Gone. Myspace: May as well be gone. The specific circumstances of each company's demise are different, but the underlying reason is the same: past success led to future failure. In a rapidly changing world, the problems they solved were irrelevant. They were asking the wrong questions and solving the wrong problems.

Many great companies fail because their leaders believe they are too great to be dethroned. I've heard executives say, "Well, that may have happened to Sears, but it won't happen to us. We are different."

No, we aren't. In fact, things are more challenging today than they were back when Sears was the top dog.

Success requires checking our egos at the door. Around the corner, there is someone who is confident they can make us irrelevant. And given past evidence, I would put my money on the new entrant, not on the incumbent.

If we are complacent or arrogant, we will assume that we have all of the answers. But maybe we have answers to unimportant questions. Just because we *knew* our industry doesn't mean we *know* our industry. We need to challenge our assumptions and ask more relevant questions.

> Just because we knew our industry doesn't mean we know our industry.

When we know a topic well, it makes it difficult for us to think differently about it. If you spent the past thirty years in your industry, the questions you ask and the ideas you develop are most likely based on your past experience rather than on current realities. This means you're probably asking the wrong questions. And when you ask the wrong questions, you solve the wrong problems, which leads to irrelevant solutions.

The world around us is not changing incrementally; it's evolving at an exponential rate. To succeed in the future, the pace of change inside our organizations needs to be faster than the pace outside. And the quality of our questions needs to keep evolving at that pace.

This is why the World Economic Forum's most recent five-year outlook reported that the single most important skill for organizations and individuals to have today is "complex problem-solving." "Critical thinking" and "creativity" came in at numbers two and three, respectively. As technologies like artificial intelligence continue to advance, complex problem-solving, creativity, and other soft skills are becoming the foundation required for success. The report notes that,

"[i]t's true that AI can solve problems that humans

cannot—but it also goes the other way. When problem-solving needs to span multiple industries or when problems are not fully defined, humans can work backwards to figure out a solution."

The need for these important skills is reinforced by an analysis of the most in-demand soft-skill of 2019, which, according to LinkedIn, is creativity, of which problem-solving is a core component.

Although the World Economic Forum report suggests that complex problem-solving is the most critical skill required in business today, I would argue that complex problem-formulation is even more important. If we ask the wrong questions, we will never get the right answers. The key is having the right questions formulated in the right way, which leads to better problem-solving and better, faster, and cheaper solutions.

People Don't Want Creativity

Although most leaders would agree that change and creativity are necessary to remain competitive, it doesn't mean they really embrace either. Even if your organization tells you that they want you to be more creative, you shouldn't necessarily believe it.

A study conducted by Jack Goncalo, assistant professor of organizational behavior at Cornell University's School of Industrial and Labor Relations (ILR), showed that most people won't recognize a creative idea if it smacks them in the face. And to compound matters, it demonstrated they really don't want creative ideas; there is a strong subconscious anticreativity bias that can interfere with one's ability to recognize a creative idea. In other words, people say they want creativity when, deep down inside, they fight it.

To uncover this bias against creativity, Goncalo and his team used a technique called the Implicit Association Test (IAT). This tool, developed by Harvard University, has been used by researchers interested in studying implicit attitudes and stereotypes ranging from political beliefs to preferences for certain social groups over others to the more nonsocial side of life, including preferences for different-flavored soft drinks.

Because it truly tests subconscious beliefs, implicit associations often are not consistent with what an individual says. In fact, this particular study revealed something very interesting: While people explicitly claimed to desire creative ideas, when using the IAT, they subconsciously associated creativity with negative words such as "agony," "poison," and "vomit."

Goncalo said this bias caused subjects to reject ideas for new products that were novel and high quality. Novelty is often viewed as being antithetical to practicality. Practicality equals value. Newness, on the other hand, carries the subconscious implication of uncertainty, which feels dangerous to survival. This creates tension in the evaluator's mind, which leads him to choose the safe solution over riskier, yet more creative ones.

Uncertainty drives the search for and generation of creative ideas, but it "also makes us less able to recognize creativity, perhaps when we need it most," the researchers wrote. "Revealing the existence and nature of a bias against creativity can help explain why people might reject creative ideas and stifle scientific advancements, even in the face of strong intentions to the contrary."

So, we have a daunting task: We need to solve problems, but the brain fights anything new. We need an approach that makes the change feel less risky and more understandable. Interestingly, sometimes the best way to find solutions to a problem is to avoid looking for solutions. Instead of focusing on the endpoint, we need to start at the beginning: the question. And the lenses in this book can help bring that clarity.

66

Changing just one word in a problem statement can reveal a completely new range of solutions.

CHAPTER 2

What's the Impact of Poor Questions?

Imagine you're serving on the jury of an only-child custody case following a relatively messy divorce. The facts of the case are complicated by ambiguous economic, social, and emotional considerations. You need to base your decision entirely on the following observations:

- Parent A has an average income, average health, average working hours, a reasonable rapport with the child, and a relatively stable social life. This parent is essentially average in every way. Plain vanilla. Nothing bad and nothing overly positive.
- Parent B, on the other hand, has an above-average income, minor health problems, a lot of work-related travel, a very close relationship with the child, and an extremely active social life. This parent has both notable strengths and notable weaknesses.

According to the researchers who conducted this study:

- If the jury is asked who should get custody, most people choose Parent B.
- If the jury is asked who should not get custody, most people choose Parent B (which, by default, means that Parent A would be awarded custody).

Simply adding one word to the question changed people's responses and beliefs. What's going on here?

When asked who should get custody, people look for the positive attributes and see that Parent B has more positive attributes than the blander Parent A. Conversely, when asked who should not get custody, people look for the negative attributes and see that Parent B has more negative attributes.

One word in a question can have a huge impact on the thought process and therefore on the range of solutions. For example, when NASA was addressing the challenge of dirty clothes in space, they found one word made all the difference. Asking, "How can we *get* clothes clean?" yielded solutions around cleaning fluids. But "How can we *keep* clothes clean?" provided different responses. In this case, the solution became a material science problem involving clothing with built-in antimicrobials.

Questions are powerful. And the words we choose for them are critical, because changing just one word can completely change your answers.

Questions Impact Your Thought Process

Not only can the wording of a question affect the type of solutions you develop, the phrasing also can affect your thought process, which will affect the speed of finding a solution.

To illustrate, let's start with a simple example. It doesn't matter how closely you follow college sports—everyone knows about March

Madness, the NCAA basketball playoffs. Ignoring the First Four qualifying games, sixty-four teams compete in total.

Sixty-four teams compete with the hope of making it into the Sweet Sixteen, the Elite Eight, and the Final Four before ultimately being crowned the champion. The tournament is single elimination—i.e., after each game, the winner advances to the next round and the loser is eliminated.

Here's the question: "How many games must be played in order to determine which team is the champion?"

Some creative people suggest the answer is one: the final game. I love that solution. But in this case, I really want to know how many games are being played. Put another way, if I wanted to buy tickets to each and every game, how many tickets would I have to buy?

The way most people find the answer is to draw out the full bracket and count the number of games in the chart. As a result, when I ask groups this question, it takes time for everyone to arrive at an answer. Interestingly, most people still get it wrong!

However, if I were to phrase the question differently, you might instantly discover the solution.

Instead of "How many games must be played in order to determine which team is the champion?" what if I asked "How many games must be played in order to eliminate all of the losers?"

The answer should now be obvious: If you have sixty-four teams playing, sixty-three teams must lose. Right? Since the tournament is single elimination, sixty-three games must be played to eliminate all of the losers. Therefore, sixty-three games must be played in order to determine the remaining team that is the champion.

This simple exercise makes an incredibly important point: The way you phrase a problem will lead you through a particular thought process. With this example, changing the question did not change the solution, but it did change the speed at which we arrived at the solution.

Asking the right question in the right way is the surest way to accelerate finding better solutions. Sometimes a tiny change can have a significant impact on the way you view the problem; often you just need to look at it from a different perspective.

Questions Impact Your Emotional State

Questions not only affect the solutions and thought process—they also can impact emotional response.

> Questions not only affect the solutions and thought process—they also can impact emotional response.

In 2003, I moved from London to Boston and decided to invest in the best mattress I could find. In my opinion, a high-quality bed is always a great investment.

Ten years later, I still had the same mattress, which was as comfortable as ever. Whenever a television commercial counselled me to "Buy our mattress and get the best night's sleep," it might have made me sleepy, but I wasn't convinced I should buy a new mattress.

Then one day, I turned on the television and saw a commercial from a local store, Jordan's Furniture. The spokesperson, Elliott, pulled out a vacuum cleaner and started vacuuming a mattress. As he did so, he asked, "Did you know you should replace your mattress every eight years? Why? It's simple. Even though your eight-year-old mattress may look okay, it doesn't mean it is. In eight years, it practically doubles in weight due to sweat, dead skin cells, and millions of dust mites."

He then emptied the vacuum canister, which was filled with dirt and grime. *Gross!*

Which commercial had me buying a new mattress? Best night's sleep or millions of dust mites?

The first mattress company was solving the problem asked by the question "How can we convince people that our beds will give them a good night's sleep?" Jordan's Furniture solved the problem prompted by the question "How can we convince people that their current mattress might be unhealthy?" The goal was the same: sell mattresses. But the problem statements were different. And in this case, changing the question changed the emotional state.

During a speech a few years back, I told this story in an old, classic theater in the Nashville, Tennessee, area. It was a gorgeous theater, but it was showing its age. It was ready for another renovation. When I said, "If my bed weighed twice its original weight after just eight years, can you imagine what's going on in the seats in this theater?" At that point, a half dozen people screamed and ran out of the theater.

Questions are powerful. They impact not just the solution and thought process, but also how we feel. Unfortunately, we tend to ask questions that are not effective or impactful.

66

Our questions can be powerful tools for learning, but only if they challenge our assumptions rather than confirm our beliefs.

CHAPTER 3

Why Do We Ask Terrible Questions?

Imagine this scenario: A woman walks into a hardware store. She can buy six for $6, twelve for $12, or twenty-four for $12. What type of item is she purchasing?

I've asked this question to thousands of executives over the years, and no one has immediately ever gotten the correct solution (unless they've heard it before). There's not enough information for them to find a proper answer, so I allow them to ask me any number of yes/no questions, sort of like in the old game *Twenty Questions*.

The first questions people inevitably ask are:

- Is the item metal?
- Is it a BOGO—buy one, get one free?
- Do you use it to attach something to something else, like a screw or nail?

The list has become quite predictable. Why? People form a solution in their mind and then ask questions to validate it. Their questions really are designed only to prove what they already suspect is true.

Most people do this often, both professionally and personally. Sometimes this is done in order to lead the witness, meaning we have an agenda and our question is designed to get another person to agree with us. "Would you like to go to McDonald's tonight for dinner?" is a closed-ended (i.e., yes or no) question that leads to one solution: fast food. A nonleading, open-ended question like "What would you like to eat for dinner tonight?" might give rise to several possibilities. But if you have your heart set on a Big Mac, you might get an answer you don't like.

In other cases, we ask predictable questions because we jump to conclusions and then ask questions that support our hypotheses. Using the hardware store example above, if you think the answer is a ruler, you might ask "Does it have anything to do with measurement?" (In case you are wondering, it doesn't.)

How do you overcome this tendency? One key is to pause and ask yourself "What assumptions am I making? What do I believe to be true?" Consider the possibility that your assumptions aren't true and work from there.

Another way is to ask nonleading questions that truly are designed to gather more information rather than to confirm your existing beliefs. With the example above, no one ever asks "Is forty-eight $12?" But from my perspective, this should be the next logical question. Instead of jumping to conclusions, I am now in a position to get more data. Since forty-eight does, in fact, cost $12, the next logical question might be "Is ninety-six $12?" Again, the answer is yes.

When I demonstrate this form of questioning, people become intrigued. They had not thought about asking questions this way. They get excited. Often the next question is "Is there any number that costs more than $12?" Yes! Ninety-seven is $12. Ninety-eight is $12. Ninety-nine is $12. But one hundred is not $12.

Armed with this new information, someone inevitably gets the correct answer: house numbers. Each number costs $6. Therefore, the number 6 (or 0, 1, 2, 3, 4, 5, 7, 8, or 9) is $6. The number 12 is two numbers—1 and 2—so it totals up to $12. At three figures, 100 costs $18—$6 for each number.

At this point, there is a collective sigh of relief that the puzzle has finally been solved. Closure. And most of the audience wants to run me out of town.

Although the exercise can be a bit painful for some, it makes a powerful point that people don't quickly forget: Our questions can be powerful tools for learning, but only if they challenge our assumptions rather than confirm our beliefs.

> Our questions can be powerful tools for learning, but only if they challenge our assumptions rather than confirm our beliefs.

The Brain Is Wired for Survival

Why do we make assumptions?

The quick answer is because the brain is wired primarily for survival.

The brain says to itself, "Everything I've done in the past has kept me alive, so I must be doing something right." Therefore, it wants to perpetuate the past. Past experiences equal safety. As a result, the brain creates neural pathways—sort of like information superhighways—to things we have thought about for a long time or things we think about on a regular basis.

For example, if I asked you to quickly name a color, odds are you would choose red, blue, green, or yellow. (From my experience, more than 50 percent of people will choose red or blue.) Why? Because these are typically the first colors we learned as children. We have known these colors the longest, so we have the deepest neural pathways to them.

Deep neural pathways can lead us to develop snap judgments based on our past experiences. This isn't necessarily bad. The problem arises when, once those assumptions are formed, we fail to challenge them.

Imagine the last time you lost something—for example, your keys. Recall the experience. You looked everywhere: in your dirty laundry, on your desk, in your handbag, in your briefcase. After fifteen minutes, you eventually found your keys. What did you inevitably say to yourself? "Can you believe it? They were in the last place I looked!"

Of course! Who finds something and keeps on looking for it? That is ridiculous! The same is true with the brain: Once the brain has formulated an opinion or assumption, it is wired to take action.

> The more you know about your business, industry, function, spouse, family, and friends, the more assumptions you make.

If you were back in caveman days and you saw an animal that was furry, had long fangs, and looked like a saber-toothed cat, odds are you would not analyze it further. You would get the heck out of there. Of course, in that situation, running away is a great strategy. But in business, moving quickly in the wrong direction can take you further from your ultimate objectives.

When we combine assumptions with a desire for immediate action, we often end up moving quickly in the wrong direction. This explains why change is often so difficult for most people: It's risky, and it threatens our survival. It is why we need to challenge our assumptions and reframe our questions.

The Brain Rewards Assumptions

Identifying assumptions is not easy. That's because the more you know about your business, industry, function, spouse, family, and friends, the more assumptions you make. These assumptions create blind spots that prevent you from seeing what is really going on. In order to ask the right questions, you need to shine a light on those blind spots.

Assumptions are beliefs that we hold to be true, oftentimes regardless of the facts. The key is to bring these assumptions to the surface in order to confirm or refute their validity. If you don't, your questions might be overly influenced by past experiences, potentially leading you in the wrong direction.

It happens to companies all of the time. Kodak, for example, assumed it was a film company—in fact, it was in the business of capturing moments and sharing experiences. This led the company to ignore any non-film solutions, such as digital camera innovations, until it was too late. This, in spite of the fact that they invented the digital camera in the 1970s.

If it can happen to them, it can happen to us.

Why do we hold on to faulty assumptions? Because the brain is wired to convince us we are right, even when we are wrong. A psychological phenomenon called confirmation bias causes us to ignore information that is inconsistent with our beliefs. Bad news and contradicting evidence are disregarded.

Why?

According to research conducted by Bojana Kuzmanovic of the Max Planck Institute for Metabolism Research in Cologne, any time we hear information that supports our assumptions, the brain activates two areas of the prefrontal cortex associated with other rewards, like food and money. We look for information that supports our beliefs because we receive a reinforcing boost when we find it. Even when we are 99 percent wrong, the brain looks for the 1 percent so it can say, "Hey, you were right about this decision. Congratulations!" This is why beliefs are so difficult to shift—the brain loves to be correct. It will give us the equivalent of an adrenalin rush, even when we are wrong.

Interestingly, the study also concluded that "[t]he influence of preferences is independent of expertise. We can benefit from this pleasant self-strengthening effect as long as our judgments do not have serious consequences." This implies that even when we have little experience, our confidence levels might be overly inflated. That said, the study concludes, "[w]hen making important decisions, we should be aware of our tendency to distort judgment and apply strategies to increase objectivity."

This is great advice. Simply being aware of these biases is a good first step; remind yourself and others that we all have these tendencies and that ego and arrogance lead to bad decision-making. A willingness to be wrong is critical for reducing failure rates. You know the old saying about what happens when you assume.

The Twenty-Five Lenses

How do we systematically challenge our assumptions? Fortunately, you are holding one solution in your hands. Using the twenty-five lenses offered in this book to reframe your challenges will help you bring your assumptions to the surface. The process of reframing requires that you systematically question the direction you are going.

To help you sift through the lenses, they are grouped into five categories, with five lenses per category:

1. Lenses that reduce abstraction (Chapter 5): Use these to make questions more specific when they are too broad.

1. LEVERAGE
2. DECONSTRUCT
3. REDUCE
4. ELIMINATE
5. HYPONYM

2. Lenses that increase abstraction (Chapter 6): Use these to make questions less specific if the challenge is too narrowly defined.

6. ANALOGY
7. RESULT
8. CONCERN REFRAME

9. STRETCH

10. HYPERNYM

3. Lenses that change perspective (**Chapter 7**)**:** Use these when you need to look at the question with a fresh set of eyes.

11. RESEQUENCE

12. REASSIGN

13. ACCESS

14. EMOTION

15. SUBSTITUTE

4. Lenses that switch elements (**Chapter 8**)**:** Use these when you have multiple factors that can be swapped.

16. FLIP

17. CONFLICTS

18. PERFORMANCE PARADOX

19. PAIN VS GAIN

20. BAD IDEA

5. Lenses that help you zero-in on an opportunity (**Chapter 9**)**:** Use these to ensure that you are asking the best question to help solve your problem.

21. REAL PROBLEM

22. REAL BUSINESS

23. INSIGHTS

24. VARIATIONS

25. OBSERVATION

To make it easy to spot the lenses within the text, they are always listed in capital letters.

Questioning Your Assumptions

The lenses discussed in this book will help you bring to the surface assumptions that might exist in your problem statements and allow you to look at situations from different angles. But where do you find the problems to solve? Sometimes bringing assumptions to the surface can help you find opportunities that you didn't even know existed.

The first step to identifying your assumptions is to list them. What are your assumptions about your organization, your industry, your competitors, your customers, or your products? One simple clue to an assumption is when people say "We always do it this way" or "We never do it that way"—that "it" often belies an assumption. Keep in mind that every assumption has a genealogy. Once you identify one, it is often insightful to ask "What are the underlying assumptions of this assumption?" as well.

Another great way to capture assumptions is through storytelling. Let's say you're redesigning a car. You might start by asking "What do we know to be true about a car?" Cars have four wheels, a steering wheel, windshield wipers, an engine, and a space for the driver. Tell the full and elaborate story. A car has four wheels. Does it need four wheels? What if it had three wheels? What's the upside? What if it had five wheels? It has a steering wheel. Autonomous vehicles in the future probably won't have steering wheels. What about windshield wipers? Maybe a wiper isn't the best way to eliminate the rain from a car's windshield. Or maybe we redefine how we develop windshield wipers.

Ask employees and customers to tell stories as well. Record the conversations and get them transcribed. Highlight the sentences that might imply underlying assumptions. Be sure to take your time with this. The most dangerous assumptions are implicit, not explicit.

Once you have a list of assumptions, force the opposite to be true. What if what you believe to be true isn't? What are the implications of that? What would you do differently? For anything that you don't believe to be true, what if it actually is? What would you need to do moving forward to address this? How would it change you? Forcing the opposite to be true is not easy and takes time. Don't rush through it. Give each assumption proper consideration. Afterward, discern and validate which are correct and which need to be busted.

The Lenses and Assumptions

Let's fold all of this into a simple example that demonstrates how you can apply this technique—and the lenses—to your business.

Imagine you run a restaurant and you want to find a new way to distinguish yourself in the market. You list all of the assumptions you have about restaurants: The customer enters, sits down, and orders a meal. The order is taken, and the meal is prepared in the kitchen. Then the food is served and eaten. The bill is issued and paid. After the customer leaves, someone cleans the table.

First, let's look at some underlying assumptions and questions, regardless of whether they are true. Several assumptions typically are made about eating in restaurants:

- We assume that people like to eat in restaurants.
- We assume that part of the appeal of a restaurant is the desire to be waited on—i.e., to have someone else do the work of cooking, serving, and cleaning.
- We assume that everyone wants something different, hence the menu of choices.
- We assume that people want to know what they are paying in advance of ordering.

There are undoubtedly many other assumptions at work here. Let's look at applying a few of the lenses.

The REASSIGN lens (#12) could help move work to the customers. What could customers do? They could get their own soft drinks and bus their own trays. They could choose their own food from a salad bar or buffet, eliminating the need for waitstaff. You can take it a step further and have the customers cook their own food, which is a trendy concept at some restaurants. Of course, there are numerous home delivery kits now for the customers to do the cooking in their own homes. And delivery companies like Grubhub and Uber Eats reassign who delivers the meal to the customer.

The RESEQUENCE lens (#11) could affect when the food is cooked. By cooking food in advance of customers arriving at the restaurant, you could predict what people will want and have it ready and waiting for them. This could include complete meals, such as what McDonald's does with the hamburgers under the warming lights. Or you could partially prepare certain commonly used components, like sauces or soups.

The ELIMINATE lens (#4) can lead to a lot of interesting results. One reasonable assumption is that menus list the prices for each item. If it is a fancy restaurant, the menus might list only whole dollar amounts, but there are still prices. Or maybe it's a *prix fixe* menu (French for "fixed price") and you don't list the price per item, but there are still prices, typically for a three- to five-course meal. Regardless, your customers usually want to know in advance what they will pay, with the price listed somewhere. But what if you completely removed prices from the menu?

A Chinese restaurant I went to in London many years ago listed no prices on the menu. At the end of the meal, customers were given a silver tray and asked to leave what they thought the meal was worth. The restaurant owners trusted that customers would pay a reasonable amount for what they ate. Did they lose money by doing this?

As it turned out, the restaurant owners had secretly priced each item and compared the money the diners left behind at the end of their meals to what they would have charged if they had listed prices. Interestingly, they calculated that, on average, they received slightly more money when they removed the prices from the menus. And their business increased because this was such a clever idea.

Bring your assumptions to the surface. Use the lenses to help you reframe your assumptions. Let go of your ego. Allow yourself to be wrong. Do not let confirmation bias elevate only your faulty assumptions. Not challenging assumptions can severely impact your business—and your life.

With that as backdrop, let's move into the lenses.

TWENTY-FIVE LENSES FOR REFRAMING PROBLEMS

66

Although reframing questions won't feel natural at first, when you use the problem-formulation lenses, it will become easier over time. It's like building a muscle.

CHAPTER 4

About the Lenses

The way questions are worded is incredibly important. Changing just one word in a question can bring us a completely different range of solutions. Shifting from "How can we speed up the bags?" to "How can we slow down the passengers?" to "How can we reduce wait time?" to "How can we improve the wait experience?" will lead to fundamentally different answers.

Saying we should reframe questions is easy; actually *doing* it is difficult. Through years of innovation work, I've found that most people struggle with reframing questions, but doing it well is crucial for success. This is why I developed my problem-formulation lenses. These lenses help you to refine a challenge statement in multiple ways.

You might find that, in the beginning, this process is not easy. In fact, you might get frustrated at first (remember the house numbers activity from chapter 3?). Using the lenses and reframing questions won't feel natural at first, because it's not how most of us are wired. Although it might seem daunting, it is actually quite exciting. When you and your team see what is truly possible, everyone will fall in love with asking the right questions. Fortunately, the process becomes easier over time, like building a muscle. You even will find that some individuals (about 5 to 10 percent of the workforce) do this naturally without needing the lenses. Get them actively involved in the process. They will enjoy it and you will get a lot of value. As you get better at asking the right questions the right way, you will see results multiply quickly.

There are twenty-five lenses in this book grouped into five categories. This is far from an exhaustive list. Feel free to create your own lenses. Catalog your examples. Share them with others. I even encourage you to share your newly found lenses and examples with me.

Using the Lenses

Using the lenses is simple. Just read them and see which ones apply to your situation. You will find the "Lenses Cheat Sheet" on the fold-out insert and "Challenge Template" and other materials in the Supporting Resources section at the back of the book. The cheat sheet will help you quickly navigate all of the lenses, while the template provides a structured way for you to write down your challenges. Once you have this book, the cheat sheet, and the challenge template, it is time to begin.

Identify an issue, problem, opportunity, or challenge that you want to address. Don't worry if the question is important—we are only practicing for now. As you better understand the process, you will improve at choosing the right challenges. As always, be sure to bring your assumptions to the surface.

Write down your challenge statement on the first line of the template.

All good challenges start with "How can we . . ." You may have heard that challenge statements should start with "How might we . . ." Although from a linguistic perspective they are equivalent, I find "can" more natural in conversation. Regardless, be sure to avoid "How do we . . ."; that structure is less about possibility and more about action and getting things done. This might seem like nitpicking, but remember that changing one word can significantly impact your thought process.

Sometimes you might find that you want to ask a "selection" question. These typically begin with "Which . . ." Depending on the situation, this might be an acceptable way to ask your question. If you are looking to choose the best place to stay, for example, instead of asking "How can we find the best hotel?" it is more convenient to ask "Which hotel is best for us?" Of course, these two questions are not synonymous, because the "how can we" version suggests finding a process, whereas the "which" question implies finding the actual place.

Equally, you might ask "When . . ." or "Who . . ." questions. Keep in mind that these could reduce the range of possible solutions, as they imply only one dimension of a question. Use your judgment. "How can we" is a framework, not a rule. Having said that, you should avoid asking binary questions (e.g., "Should we . . ." or "Can we . . ."), which provide only yes or no answers.

Once you develop your first iteration of your "How can we" question, you can apply lenses to help you reframe it. Review the cheat sheet to see which lenses fit best. Or, better yet, try all of the lenses and force them to fit. You will find that every lens can be applied to any challenge, though some are a bit more difficult.

Write down as many variations as you can. Try to do it at least six times. A half dozen variations using at least six lenses. More is better, as it stretches your thinking.

There are a couple of things to look out for as you go through this process. For starters, avoid jumping to solutions. It is so tempting to try to find answers before you have created a great list of questions: Stay in the challenge formulation phase.

Also, it is valuable to apply one lens more than one time to a given problem. It is all too easy to find a quick reframe and move on. It takes more discipline to find multiple variations from a single lens. Have patience.

In addition, recognize that questions beget more questions. Sometimes when you ask a question, you might need to answer another question in order to move forward. For example, if you originally asked "How can we target our most profitable customers?" your next logical question might be "Who are our most profitable customers?" I call these data-gathering questions "insight questions" (as opposed to "challenge questions"). Although answering an insight question might not provide a solution, it should provide information that will help you further reframe your primary question.

The point is that it is important to practice reframing. As you go through this process, ask which of the reframed questions seems to create the greatest results. Play around with it. Different questions will lead to different solutions, which will result in different levels of value.

The Lens Structure

Each lens contains four pieces of information:

Identifier (Name and Brief Description)—This is a quick way to refer to a lens, as it helps you browse through them and find ones that you've read before. Each lens has a name and short descriptor to help you remember it.

When to Use This Lens—This information will help you quickly determine which lenses might be the best fit for your particular challenge. Sometimes it is useful to start looking here.

How to Use This Lens—This shows you how to use the lens and provides details about its application. Sometimes it includes questions you can ask. Sometimes it provides perspectives you can take.

Example(s) of This Lens in Action—It is always easiest to understand how to use a lens when you see how it was applied to another problem statement. Although many of the examples are business related, you will find that the concepts apply to all types of problems in life.

As previously mentioned, the twenty-five lenses are organized into five different categories. These are designed to help you find the best lenses for your particular situation.

When questions are overly broad, use the Reduce Abstraction lenses. When they are overly specific, use the Increase Abstraction lenses. The Switch Elements lenses are useful when there are multiple parameters associated with a problem. The Zero-In and Change Perspective lenses should always be considered.

Each of the remaining chapters in this section represent the different categories. The first page of each chapter contains a pair of glasses. Right below it will be a symbol with the name of the lens category next to it. The symbol links back to the part of the framework you see below. For example, the down arrow represents the Reduce Abstraction lenses whereas the two horizontal arrows indicate the Switch Elements lenses.

With that as background, let's dig in and start using the lenses to help you uncover hidden solutions to your most difficult problems.

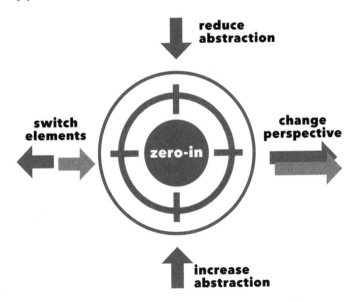

reduce abstraction

#1 Leverage

#2 Deconstruct

#3 Reduce

#4 Eliminate

#5 Hyponym

CHAPTER 5

Reduce Abstraction

The lenses designed to reduce abstraction are geared toward making questions more specific when they are too broad. When your challenge statement is overly large, broad, or abstract, these lenses will help you bring it down to earth.

#1: Leverage
Solve for the Greatest Impact

Use This Lens When . . . Your Question Is Too Abstract

When you're asking overly abstract questions, like "How can we increase revenues?" or "How can we improve productivity?" identifying the leverage points can kick-start the problem-solving process. It allows you to focus on what will return the greatest value with the least amount of investment. Then, after you solve for the first leverage point, you can work on the next one.

How to Use This Lens

Ask:
- What is the one factor that will have the greatest impact?
- What gives us the greatest leverage in solving this challenge?
- What's the most important factor in driving change?
- If we could only solve one aspect of this problem, what would give us the greatest result?

Answering these questions often requires data or analysis. For example, you might want to identify which target markets or customers have the greatest impact. Or which products are creating the highest margins. Or, if your goal is to improve productivity, you might want to identify the areas of the business that are the least efficient. The key is to find the factor that yields the largest results with the least amount of effort. Gather the data you need to answer the question.

Example of This Lens in Action

A nonprofit in the United Kingdom asked "How can we fix the education system?" Previous attempts to do this had failed because the problem was too abstract and had too many areas for improvement: teacher quality, teachers' pay, class size, technology, curriculum, nutrition, and much more.

The first step in solving the problem was to apply the RESULT lens (#7). Recognizing that education is a means to an end, they asked "What's the outcome of education?" A child's learning is certainly one. Starting with this problem led them to ask a leverage question: "What is the one factor that has the greatest impact on a child's learning?" As it turns out, it has been scientifically proven that the answer is positive parental involvement. Solving for this problem, "How can we create an environment of positive parental involvement?" led to a workable solution. This example also demonstrates that you often need to use multiple lenses in order to find a hidden solution.

#2: Deconstruct
Break into Smaller Parts

Use This Lens When . . . a Broad Challenge Has No
Clear Leverage Point

As we saw with the Goldilocks Principle, overly abstract challenges invite high quantities of low-value or irrelevant solutions. This results in wasted energy during the submission, problem-solving, and evaluation phases (see chapter 11). When there is no obvious leverage point, deconstructing a problem into smaller pieces will reduce abstraction.

How to Use This Lens

Break your challenge into multiple smaller challenges. There are several ways to do this.
Ask:
- What are the parts or components of this? (For example, if you are working on a car, it could be wheels, windshield, and seats.)
- What are the steps of the process? (These could include order processing, shipping, and returns.)
- What are the different segments, such as customer groups, demographics, psychographics, and geography?

When deconstructing a problem, be sure to account for inter-dependencies. Otherwise, you might solve one problem while creating another. For example, an electronics manufacturer optimized its production process so that it could turn out finished goods in four hours, yet they didn't account for the impact on shipping and order entry. In the end, inventory levels increased and there was no net benefit to the company or its customers. Never solve a deconstructed problem in isolation.

Examples of This Lens in Action

A hotel chain initially worked on the challenge "How can we improve the guest experience?" This invited a lot of ideas, but none was considered to be of high value. They broke the business into the parts of the process, including check-in, room service, housekeeping, and check-out. They decided that making a great first and last impression were critical for the satisfaction of the entire stay. So, they invested heavily in solving the challenge "How can we improve the check-in/check-out experience?" This is an example of deconstructing by process steps.

A financial services company deconstructed its call center operations by complexity of incoming calls. Simple calls were those that could be completed within three minutes and handled by an entry level employee. All other calls were categorized as complex and were only handled by paid specialists. They determined that 60 percent of the calls were indeed simple and could be performed by their least expensive resources. Given this information, they asked "How can we make our simple calls as efficient as possible?" By optimizing the most frequent scenario, they were able to reduce costs by over 50 percent. Sometimes the process of deconstructing can help you find the leverage point.

#3: Reduce
Drop Expectations or Simplify

Use This Lens When . . . Complexity and Stretch
Targets Are Not Producing the Desired Results

More is not always better. Sometimes setting goals too high
causes dysfunctional behavior. [See the PERFORMANCE
PARADOX lens (#18) for more about this.] A short-sighted devo-
tion to hitting targets can inadvertently hurt the business and
limit potential longer-term growth. And surprisingly, a myopic
focus on making solutions more sophisticated can sometimes
reduce their appeal to customers.

How to Use This Lens

Ask:
- How might lowering our goals and expectations
  give us a better result?
- How can reducing a target create new opportunities
  for growth?
- How can simplification increase usability and
  accessibility?

Examples of This Lens in Action

A sporting goods manufacturer had a goal of selling $1
million of inventory during a large event. They quickly sold
$900,000 and made a huge profit. But the team was determined
to sell $1 million, no matter what. Unfortunately, in order to sell
that last $100,000, they gave so many incentives to buyers that

they experienced lower overall profitability. To counterbalance the stretch revenue goal, moving forward, they decided to include a profitability goal. The combination of the two balancing measures helped the company increase margins by nearly 50 percent the following year, even though sales were slightly down.

An example of how lowering expectations can enhance creativity comes from a soap manufacturer that had 30 percent marketshare of deodorant soap—nearly one third of the market. Although the company could have asked "How can we grow our deodorant soap business beyond 30 percent?" they instead asked "How can we reinvent ourselves to capture one twentieth of a larger market?" In effect, they were asking "How can we reduce our market share to 5 percent?" Such a strategy might not require the company to sell even one more bar of soap. Instead, it could direct them toward getting a much smaller share of the much bigger toiletries market. Notice that in this case, when they reduced the target (from 30 percent to 5 percent), they actually broadened the question (from soap to toiletries).

Traditionally, console video game manufacturers focused on increasing the sophistication of their graphics and the complexity of the games. Then, Nintendo simplified the user interface with the introduction of its Wii system. With streamlined graphics and advanced controllers, anyone from eight to eighty years old could enjoy their games. When first introduced, the Wii outsold PlayStation and Xbox combined. Of course, now this concept has gone even further, as mobile games (many with extremely simple user interfaces) account for over half of all worldwide gaming revenue, surpassing sales of console and computer-based games.

#4: Eliminate
Get Rid of It

Use This Lens When . . . an Activity Does Not
Produce Sufficient Value

Instead of improving an activity, evaluate if you can stop doing
it altogether. Is there a way you could completely eliminate it
without experiencing a negative result? As Peter Drucker once
said, "There is nothing so useless as doing effectively that which
should not be done at all." Or consider Antoine de Saint-Exupéry,
author of *The Little Prince*, who once said, "Perfection is finally
attained not when there is no longer anything to add but when
there is no longer anything to take away."

How to Use This Lens

Any time you ask a question designed to improve a product
or process, first ask:

- How can this be eliminated altogether?

This can be used in so many situations. For example, if you
are looking to leverage technology to solve a problem, first ask
"What would be the result if we didn't use any technology?"

It is quite common to ask "What features can we add?" It is
less common to ask "Which features can we remove/eliminate?"
This second question is the right question, because it will lead to
a better design with increased usability.

Examples of This Lens in Action

For years, automotive manufacturers faced a bottleneck in their accounts payable process. Matching receipts and processing invoices from their vendors were time-consuming activities. One car company completely eliminated these processes. Now, the manufacturer pays suppliers only for what it uses when it uses it, not for what it receives. No matching is required, as they track only what goes on the car. When the vehicle leaves the plant, they know it has four tires, and that's when payment is issued to the tire vendor.

An extreme and controversial example comes from the tobacco industry. Instead of asking "How can we sell more cigarettes when health concerns are reducing consumption?" Philip Morris International (PMI) took a counterintuitive approach. They decided to solve the problem "How can we exit the cigarette business altogether?" Today, cigarettes account for nearly all of their revenue, so that's a pretty substantial change. To move in this direction, they invested $4.5 billion in the development of iQOS, a device that heats tobacco rather than burning it, significantly reducing the toxins released. Although it had been available in other countries for several years, in April 2019, the FDA approved the device for sale in the United States.

#5: Hyponym
Use More Specific Words

Use This Lens When . . . the Words in Your Problem Are Too Broad

Unlike the DECONSTRUCT lens (#2), which is used to break an issue into smaller parts, this lens focuses on changing the wording to narrow the range of focus.

How to Use This Lens

Ask:

- Is there a more specific instance of a word that can replace the one originally chosen?

This is a hyponym. Think of it as a "type" of a given word. Hyponyms for flowers, for example, include roses, perennials, and artichokes (yes, an artichoke technically is a flower). Using a hyponym reduces abstraction, thus reducing the possible solution set. This makes it easier for you to target and find what will best serve your needs, eliminating irrelevant options.

Examples of This Lens in Action

If you were a restaurateur, for example, your original question might be "How can we attract more customers?" Hyponyms for "customer" include "patron" and "regular." Employing this lens could lead to the question "How can we attract more regulars?" which focuses the challenge on repeat business. "Subscriber" also is a hyponym of customer. Although it may seem unusual for a restaurant, an interesting question might be "How can we attract more subscribers?" Delivery services like Blue Apron do this. Emerging restaurant subscription services like MealPal allow customers to pay a flat fee for twelve meals a month at a variety of restaurants.

Hyponyms are incredibly useful for stimulating new perspectives. For example, if you are working on the problem "How can we move a heavy item?" and you aren't going anywhere (pun intended), look at the list of hyponyms for "move" to inspire new thoughts: spread, carry, float, glide, fly, push, roll, and ski. Each of these would generate different problem statements. "How can we spread the heavy item?" may lead you down the path of disassembling it or even flattening it to increase the surface area. "How can we glide the heavy item?" may get you thinking about ways to reduce the friction between the ground and the item using solutions like ice or lubricants.

increase abstraction

#6 Analogy

#7 Result

#8 Concern Reframe

#9 Stretch

#10 Hypernym

CHAPTER 6

Increase Abstraction

When your challenge statement is overly specific or implies a particular solution or area of expertise, these lenses will help you expand your thinking to increase the range of possibilities.

#6: Analogy
Find Someone Similar

Use This Lens When . . . You've Been Recycling Past
Solutions

This lens is often used during the solution-finding process,
but it is also valuable during reframing. It can help you find
a kernel of a solution elsewhere by expanding a narrow area of
expertise to a broader one, thereby providing more potential
solutions.

How to Use This Lens

Reframe the question to help identify others who solved
similar but not identical problems. Ask:
- What is this like?
- Who else has solved a problem like this?

Then explore how you can adapt their solution to your situation. (See the "Shift" portion of chapter 11 for more details.)

Examples of This Lens in Action

Dental experts looking to creating a whitening toothpaste
asked "How can we make teeth whiter?" This led to typical solutions such as abrasives or bleaches. This statement was specific in
that it assumed the solution would come from dental-care experts.
They eventually reframed the question to "Who else makes whites
whiter?" which led them to explore how laundry detergent creates
the illusion of whiteness through bluing agents. The new chal-

lenge became "How can we create a toothpaste that has a blue dye in it?" The result was a toothpaste called Signal White Now, which instantly creates the illusion of white teeth.

Don't just look to other businesses. Sometimes the best solutions can be found in nature and less obvious places. Consider the gas pipeline industry, which has struggled to solve the problem "How can we find and seal cracks in pipelines?" When they asked "Who else solved a similar problem?" they realized that sealing cracks is something that the cardiovascular system's coagulation mechanisms do all of the time. Armed with this knowledge, industry experts worked on the problem "How can we create an inert coagulant ingredient that will seal small cracks?"

#7: Result
Focus on What You Are Trying to Accomplish

Use This Lens When . . . Your Question Is Focused
on a Specific Activity

The goal of this lens is to move away from solutions and toward
outcomes. By switching to outcomes, you broaden the range
of options.

How to Use This Lens

While framing the question, ask:

- What does this make possible?

This might help you find an even higher-level, more important question.

Or, instead of starting with the solution, step back and ask:

- What is the desired outcome?

Then solve for that.

Examples of This Lens in Action

Only 15 percent of a consumer goods manufacturer's
new products launched on time. They first worked on "How
can we speed up the research and development (R&D) function?" but quickly realized this was just one step of the entire
process. By working on the result-oriented "How can we speed
time-to-market?" they discovered that the delays were not caused
by R&D, but rather the back-and-forth between them and other

departments. In the end, the company created development teams that had responsibility for R&D and also responsibility for the factories, the development of marketing materials, and everything required for successful launch. Product development no longer ended at product definition; it ended three months after the marketing companies started selling the new products. By focusing on the result, now nearly 70 percent of their new products launch on time.

A major beverage company tracked the number of repair calls on its vending machines (an activity) because it was concerned about rising costs of maintaining equipment. While this revealed an interesting number, it didn't help much. It failed to show whether the company was attaining the outcome it really wanted, which was to increase the overall uptime of machines. By focusing on uptime instead, they were able to increase customer satisfaction, sales, and machine availability.

In another example, a company with a leadership development issue brainstormed "How can we more effectively use 360-degree feedback?" That's a solution masquerading as a question, so they completely missed alternative methods. When the company asked "How can we create powerful leaders?" instead, this more abstract question opened up a wider range of possible solutions. Of course, this then needed to be deconstructed into smaller and more solvable problems.

#8: Concern Reframe
Convert Concerns to Questions

Use This Lens When . . . Your Teammates Find
Reasons Solutions Won't Work

This lens is a little different than the others, because we start with a statement rather than a question. It is particularly effective at countering the "yeah, but" mentality of some individuals who look for the reasons something won't work. Use this lens whenever someone makes a statement that shuts down a conversation: "We've tried this before and it won't work." "We don't have the resources necessary to invest in this project." "Our customers won't like this." None of these are necessarily true. To help open up possible solutions, convert the statement into one or more questions.

How to Use This Lens

Ask:
- How can we take a progress-blocking statement and convert it into a question that starts with "How can we...?"

When problem-solving, inevitably someone will say "We don't have enough money," or "We don't have enough time to implement this idea." These statements imply that these are facts that can't be disputed. In response, state the concern as an opportunity: "How can we get more money?" or "How can we do this for less money?" or "How can we get it done in less time?"

Once you have a new opportunity defined, you can use any

of the other lenses to further reframe the question. Although this is a simple lens, it is an incredibly powerful way to increase creative potential. One statement can be converted into multiple questions, and what was once a "yeah but" can become a huge opportunity.

Example of This Lens in Action

A consumer goods company was strapped for resources. Every time a new idea was generated for improving their Information Technology (IT) systems, the typical response was, "We don't have enough resources to do the work." Making this statement limited their thinking and could have stopped all progress. However, when they asked "How can we do it with fewer resources?" or "How can we do it more efficiently?" they forced themselves to think harder about ways to get the work done. This ultimately led them to the questions "How can we outsource the work?" and "How can we partner with someone who has the resources?" Their ultimate solution was a creative partnering strategy that helped them get the work done quickly while reducing overall costs.

#9: Stretch
Raise Your Target

Use This Lens When . . . You're Stuck Looking at
Incremental Solutions

Sometimes you can stimulate creative thinking by increasing
your targets. Or as Jack Welch, former CEO of General Elec-
tric, once said, "The thing that is always wrong with measurements
is that you set them to a place where you can meet them." Achiev-
able goals drive incremental thinking. Stretch targets, especially
ones that are nearly impossible, require radical innovation.

How to Use This Lens

Ask:
- Are our challenge criteria stretched enough?
- Are we shooting for a high enough goal?

Try increasing your goals to stretch your thinking. If you ask
"How can we get a 5 percent improvement?" you get incremental thinking. But if you ask "How can we get a 50 percent or 100
percent improvement?" the old models of thinking won't work,
which forces you to devise new approaches and solutions.

Stretch goals are ideal during the innovation process when
you are developing solutions. However, they might not be the
right strategy for measuring day-to-day performance of employees as they can lead to the dysfunctional behaviors described
in the REDUCE lens (#3). (Wells Fargo learned this lesson when
their overly aggressive cross-sale goals led employees to open

unneeded accounts for customers, sometimes forging client sig-natures on paperwork.)

It should be noted that this lens is often used in conjunc-tion with other lenses. Once you've established a stretch target, you may need to reframe the problem again to generate better solutions.

Examples of This Lens in Action

At a large greeting-card company, cards took eighteen to twenty-four months to move from concept to store shelves. Senior executives set a stretch goal of getting new cards from concept to market in less than a year. Individual departments within the firm—designers, writers, artists, printers, shippers, and so on—believed this new stretch goal could not be met. Even so, the target became a rallying cry. In the end, the company managed to get its cards to market in only four months. The seemingly impossible goal had forced the teams to abandon their conventional approaches and to try something completely new. Previously untried forms of cross-departmental collaboration were part of the solution.

One of the most well-known examples of setting stretch goals comes from President John F. Kennedy's challenge to the United States to "put a man on the moon by the end of the decade," which sounded completely impossible to most people at the time. This stretch goal, proposed on May 25, 1961, was met on July 20, 1969, with the Apollo 11 mission.

#10: Hypernym
Use Broader Words

Use This Lens When . . . Your Problem Is Too Specific

When you use narrowly defined words, you often limit your range of thinking. Therefore, sometimes simply changing a word to one that is less specific can help you find solutions that you otherwise might have missed. These more abstract words are called hypernyms.

How to Use This Lens

Ask:

- How can we replace a word in the challenge statement with a less specific instance of the one originally chosen?

This is a hypernym, which is the opposite of a HYPONYM (lens #5). For example, dog is a hypernym for poodle, and animal is a hypernym for dog.

Examples of This Lens in Action

Tyson Foods, the world's second-largest processor and marketer of chicken, beef, and pork, recently announced that it's investing in a plant-based shellfish startup as well as vegan chicken nuggets. They've decided to move from being a "meat" company to a "protein" company. Protein is a hypernym for meat.

A natural gas company facing increased competition tried to solve the problem "How can we leverage our pipelines?" Hypernyms for "pipeline" include "conduit," "passage," and "way." This led the executives to realize that the rights-of-way used for their pipelines were a tremendous asset. They used these rights to lay fiber-optic cable and launched a new telecommunications company.

Like many authors, I asked the question "How can I write a great book?" Although this initially was the goal, I replaced the word "book" with "product"–a hypernym–to broaden the issue. This one simple word shift led to the creation of digital and physical (nonbook) products that I had not previously considered.

Hypernyms can also be useful in everyday life. Imagine you are looking to buy a new car so you can get to work. What if you swapped "car" with the hypernym "vehicle"? Now you have additional options to consider, including motorcycles, buses, and bicycles. You could take it a step further and substitute "vehicle" with the hypernym "transportation." Now you have even more options, including ride-sharing apps, hitchhiking, and teleportation. Increasing the abstraction increases the range of options.

change perspective

CHAPTER 7

Change Perspective

Sometimes you just need to look at your challenge statement with a fresh set of eyes and consider it from a different point of view.

#11: Resequence
Predict or Postpone a Decision

Use This Lens When . . . Your Challenge Implies
Timing or Sequence

The order in which activities are performed is often assumed
to be much more rigid than it actually needs to be—it is not
always as fixed as we believe. By shifting the sequencing of events,
you can potentially unleash new opportunities.

For example, if your challenge suggests that you predict
future consumption, postponing a decision could increase flex-
ibility. On the flip side, if your challenge assumes you need to
wait until you have all the necessary information before making a
decision, predicting may improve efficiency and responsiveness.
And if there are few dependencies between activities, look for
ways to perform tasks in parallel.

How to Use This Lens

When a prediction is implied, ask:
- How can we delay a decision until later in the
  process when we have more or better information?

Conversely, if your challenge implies you are postponing
action, ask:
- How can we make a decision earlier in the process,
  before we have all the necessary information?

Finally, if the activities have limited dependencies, ask:
- How can we perform multiple tasks in parallel?

The upside of postponing is you reduce waste, you more closely meet customer needs, and you reduce inventory and warehousing. The downside is a potential increase in overall lead times and costs due to a lack of economies of scale.

Conversely, predicting what you may need might increase speed and efficiency while reducing overall costs. By not waiting for all of the information to come in, you enable faster response times and improve customer service. However, you could end up having wasted resources if your predictions are wrong.

And when possible, performing activities in parallel can increase speed because multiple tasks are done at the same time.

Examples of This Lens in Action

Paint manufacturers postpone the final form of their products. Instead of "How can we predict which color paint people will buy?" they now ask "How can we mix the colors in the store when requested?" This yields less stock on the shelves, since they delay the mixing process until a customer has chosen the color.

Before accepting transferring patients, a hospital would postpone acceptance until room availability was verified. This took considerable time and sometimes resulted in patients being sent elsewhere. However, the hospital realized that it was nearly always able to find vacancies, so it began admitting patients upon request, finding and preparing rooms while those patients are in transit to the hospital. This is a great example of both predicting and parallelism in action.

#12: Reassign
Change Who Does the Work

Use This Lens When . . . Your Challenge Relies on
the Work of a Particular Person

If a problem statement implies that a particular person, department, company, or industry does the work, changing the "who"
can unleash some creative solutions. Keep in mind that sometimes the "who" can be a computer or other nonhuman. This
is a particularly powerful lens when considering the blurring of
industries' boundaries.

How to Use This Lens

There are three ways:

1. Ask "Who else could perform this task?" and substitute that person, department, organization, or industry in the question.
2. Genericize the question so that it does not imply
   anyone in particular. Allow the "who" to emerge during
   the solution finding. For example, instead of "How
   can we improve the way marketing targets customers?" you could ask "How can we (the organization as a
   whole) target customers?"
3. Reassign the work to something other than a human
   being, for example, by automating the work in
   some fashion. Ask "How else might this task be
   accomplished?"

Examples of This Lens in Action

Instead of asking "How can we get cashiers to scan faster at checkout?" some supermarkets have reassigned work by asking "How can we get customers to scan their own items?" To do this, some stores have scanners on the shopping carts or phone apps that allow customers to scan their own items as they put them in the cart. This has been taken a step further with Amazon GO, where the scanning has been reassigned to technology, eliminating the manual scanning process altogether. Their "Just Walk Out Technology" automatically detects when products are taken from or returned to the shelves and keeps track of them in a virtual cart. When you're done shopping, you just leave the store.

A large aerospace company was looking for ways to quickly deliver part kits directly to aircraft. It realized that catering trucks make deliveries to every plane, so it teamed up with a large airline catering company to provide delivery service for its parts. The company found a partner not by looking for special expertise, but by looking at how other organizations were interacting with its customers.

A fascinating example comes from Volkswagen's Resende truck and bus plant in Brazil. Traditionally, suppliers would deliver parts to a factory and leave it to the manufacturer to put together the finished product. But at this plant, major suppliers don't just deliver the components, they also assemble them inside the plant. The assembly work was reassigned to the vendor instead of the manufacturer.

#13: Access
Don't Own

If your question implies ownership of any sort, consider how giving people access to the resources might be better. In many situations, consumers are more interested in using something than owning it. The same is true of your organization; sometimes it is better to rent than own.

How to Use This Lens

Ask:
- How can we change ownership words to "access" words, such as *rent, subscribe, lease,* or *use*?

One added advantage of using this lens is that it can unveil new business models for you. For example, you might find a way to turn a product into a service that someone can subscribe to, or you might find a way to turn a service into a product that can be rented.

Examples of This Lens in Action

In the past, the music and movie industries focused on ownership, selling LPs, CDs, MP3s, and DVDs. Today, subscription streaming services like Apple Music, Spotify, Amazon Unlimited, and Netflix provide access without ownership. You pay a monthly fee for all you can consume.

This approach can be applied to physical products, too. For example, Freedom Boat Club provides unlimited access to a number of boats for a flat annual fee. You get two reservation slots. As soon as you use one, you get another. This gives everyone equal access to the boats they want, and yet does not restrict how often you can take out a boat. Nor are users limited to one boat or one location; rather, they have many to choose from. The company maintains and cleans the boats. The only additional cost to the renter is fuel. The total cost per year is often less than the cost of boat slip dues.

The same approach can be used for IT hardware. In the past, you would own your own servers. Now, you can effectively rent server space in the cloud with companies like Amazon Web Services, Microsoft Azure, and Google Cloud. The added value is that you get to expand and contract usage based on need, rather than having unused servers sitting around.

#14: Emotion
Create Questions that Generate Emotional Responses

Use This Lens When . . . Your Challenge Lacks Emotion

If your problem statement appears to fix a negative situation, consider using this lens to reframe it in a more emotional way. Don't try to correct a problem or state it as a negative. Instead, word it optimistically. However, as you will see, there are times when fixing a problem is the best way to generate an emotional response [see the PAIN VS GAIN lens (#19) for more on this].

How to Use This Lens

Ask:
- How can we shift from corrective words such as "improve," "fix," or "reduce," to a more aspirational goal?
- How can we reframe the challenge in a way that stimulates solvers from an emotional perspective?

Don't just ask questions that are about facts, data, and results (e.g., increase customer satisfaction)—ask questions that create emotional responses. Instead of "How can we improve morale?" ask "How can we get 100 percent employee engagement?" or "How can we get 5 out of 5 on employee satisfaction surveys?" Instead of asking "How can we retain our customers?" ask "How can we wow our customers?" or "How can we create customer evangelists?" or "How can we make people smile when they think of our company?" or "How can we help people feel at home when in our stores?"

Examples of This Lens in Action

Focusing on fixing problems can generate powerful emotional responses. After taking over as Walmart US CEO, Greg Foran asked employees to email him the answer to "[Where] do you think we've cut muscle instead of fat?" From the nearly 3,000 emails he received, the most common request was to put toilet seat covers back in the stores' restrooms. Foran concluded, "Small thing, but really important . . . You can never motivate anyone until you fix some of these factors." This emotion-generating question led to a series of problem-solving initiatives that were focused on improving working conditions. Although these may have seemed trivial in the scheme of things, they were all critical for getting employees on board with the broader change agenda.

A clever way to capture emotion comes from BMW's Designworks innovation studio. Several years ago, they shared the process they use to create their designs with me. Instead of starting with functions and features, designers first meet with company executives, employees, and customers to capture the emotion that customers should feel when they use the final product. Their ideas are recorded using sketch artists rather than words. Only after everyone agrees on these emotions does the design of the form and style begin. [This technique can also be applied to the OBSERVATION lens (#25).]

#15: Substitute
Replace a Word with a Similar One

Use This Lens When . . . Looking for a Fresh Perspective

This lens can be used to reframe every question. As we have already established, changing one word in a problem statement can have a profound impact on the range of solutions. This is the simplest lens, yet one of the most powerful. HYPONYM (lens #5) and HYPERNYM (lens #10) also use word substitution by changing the level of abstraction. This lens is more about shifting perspective rather than changing the level of detail.

How to Use This Lens

Ask:

- How can we swap out one or more words in the problem statement for different terms?

You can find words that are unrelated to the original words in order to completely shift the focus. You can find similar words that might have slightly different meanings or connotations. Or you can even grab a thesaurus and use synonyms.

Examples of This Lens in Action

A purchasing department initially measured its success in terms of how well it did at buying the lowest-cost items available ("How can we consistently purchase the lowest initial cost items?"). Over time, the department learned that low initial costs sometimes correlated with long lead times, less frequent deliveries, and large lot sizes—all of which contributed to increased inventory levels. The department modified its goal to track costs over the entire life cycle, shifting to "How can we consistently purchase the lowest total cost items?" Substituting "initial" with "total" resulted in a better end-to-end view of costs.

A financial services company wanted to explore new revenue generating opportunities. Instead of asking "How can we generate more sales?" they considered variations such as "How can we generate more profit?" or "How can we attract more customers?" Although "sales," "profits," and "customers" are not really synonyms, they are related, as are the terms "generate" and "attract." They all are similar words with slightly different connotations, and they revealed different solutions. The company even combined this with the REDUCE lens (#3) to yield "How can we target fewer, yet more profitable customers?" This was where they received some of the most valuable solutions.

The NASA dirty laundry challenge from chapter 2 is another great example of word substitution. By changing "How can we get clothes clean?" to "How can we keep clothes clean?" NASA yielded completely different solutions.

switch elements

CHAPTER 8

Switch Elements

Some challenge statements can be reframed simply by switching from one parameter to another. It's like the book *Eat This, Not That!* by David Zinczenko: Don't solve for "this" when you can solve for "that."

#16: Flip
Solve for a Different Factor

Use This Lens When . . . You Have Multiple
Influencing Factors

Although some situations are more obvious than others, with some work, you can often find multiple dimensions to nearly any problem statement.

How to Use This Lens

Ask:

- How can we turn the problem upside down by improving a different factor?

Many questions we want to solve have multiple components. We often get fixated on solving just one of them. But sometimes, other hidden factors can unleash a much simpler solution. We can do that by asking "Instead of fixing this factor, what if we fixed or adjusted a different factor?"

The baggage claim story from chapter 1 is a perfect example of flipping factors. Instead of speeding bags, they slowed down the passengers.

Example of This Lens in Action

Whiskey connoisseurs know that round ice has the smallest surface area and melts the slowest; it is therefore preferred over cubes. Also, the ice needs to be the right size in relation to the glass to create the ultimate experience.

A restaurant known for its fine whiskeys had a dilemma: The ice used in the drinks was too expensive to produce. The perfect ice size for their glasses was 2.5 inches in diameter. They could make 2-inch ice balls in house at no cost, but no one could find molds for making the larger size. As a result, the restaurant bought 2.5-inch ice cubes and manually shaved them down into spheres. The total cost was $30,000 a year.

The original challenge was "How can we make 2.5-inch spheres for less money?" When someone asked a different question—"How can we ensure the perfect ratio between the glass and the ice?"—another solution became obvious. Instead of reducing the cost of making 2.5-inch ice spheres, the restaurant simply bought smaller glasses, flipping the size of the ice with the size of the glass. Now the 2-inch molds worked perfectly, cutting the cost of ice to practically nothing.

#17: Conflicts
Amplify Conflicting Attributes

Use This Lens When . . . Successful Resolution Is
Determined by Multiple Influencing Factors

When problem-solving, sometimes it is useful to add some conflicting elements. This forces creative thinking that can result in clever solutions. This, like the FLIP lens (#16), works well when two or more factors influence the issue.

How to Use This Lens

Typically, we look for complementary attributes in a problem to arrive at a solution. However, to use this lens, ask:

- How can we design the challenge to allow for and embrace conflicting attributes?

This will move you from a single factor to multiple factors.

Examples of This Lens in Action

When solving the problem "How can we design a car with reduced road noise?" the obvious solution was to add extra insulation. However, today's cars require greater fuel efficiency, and the extra weight of the additional insulation can negatively impact mileage. These conflicting problems–"How can we reduce road noise?" and "How can we improve fuel efficiency?"–drove a different level of thinking. Incorporating the same kind of electronic noise cancellation technology that is installed in headphones into the design of the car added almost no extra weight, yet effectively eliminated road noise.

Imagine trying to create a ceiling paint that is white, yet clearly visible while it's being applied. These are conflicting goals, because if you are painting white on white, it can be difficult to tell if you missed a spot. Dulux's "Rolls on Pink" solved this paradoxical problem. The paint rolls on pink, yet dries bright white in thirty to sixty minutes, ensuring (in their words) "a uniform and even finish in one coat."

Or consider USAA, which provides banking, insurance, investing, and other financial services to members of the military and their families. One of their challenges was "How can members deposit checks and get access to money, even when they are not near a bank?" This geographic conflict led them to develop an app that allows their members to deposit checks by taking a picture with their cell phones—a major convenience for anyone on the road or serving overseas. Although you may enjoy a similar convenience with your bank, you can thank USAA for this innovation, as they were first to develop this approach and hold four patents for the technology.

#18: Performance Paradox
Shift Your Focus

Use This Lens When . . . You're Having Issues
Hitting a Goal

Sometimes you can improve performance by shifting your focus away from the primary objective. Don't just adjust the goal; instead, change what is measured and shift from focusing on one element to another.

How to Use This Lens

Ask:
- What can we focus on other than the outcome?

In some cases, focusing on the activity itself will improve performance. The paradox is that sometimes the best way to improve an outcome is to avoid focusing on the outcome. For example, this book illustrates that the best way to find a solution is to not focus on the solution but rather the problem.

Examples of This Lens in Action

A racecar team wanted to increase the speed at which the pit crew could change the tires, fuel the car, and perform minor maintenance. Previous attempts to get the team to work more quickly focused on telling the pit crew that they would be measured on their speed (the outcome). Paradoxically, when the pit crew members were told they would be evaluated instead on style (i.e., they were told to think "smooth"), they worked more quickly. Interestingly, all the members of the pit crew felt they were working more slowly. To go faster, they needed to stop focusing on speed.

We see the same in many areas of business. Quite often, sales reps who are measured on customer satisfaction (a present moment activity) sell more than those who are focused solely on closing a deal and sales targets (future results).

In another example, falling down is one of the leading causes of death in older people. The elderly are aware of this risk, and therefore are afraid of falling. What do they do to address their fear? They try especially hard not to fall. Ironically, trying not to fall makes them more likely to fall. By accident, an alternative solution was discovered: Teaching people to fall on purpose and then roll on the floor made them more comfortable with the idea of falling. They realized that they could indeed fall without any serious repercussions. When they lost this fear, they stopped trying not to fall. The result? They stopped falling!

#19: Pain vs Gain

Focus on Motivators

"Build it and they will come"—we hear that mantra a lot. But problem-solving can be more like "Solve a pain and they will come." When you frame a challenge as an opportunity or gain ("Wouldn't it be great if we …?"), you drive creativity but not necessarily action. Although people might be *interested* in the solution this question leads to, they may not be *driven* enough to make change happen. On the other hand, the desire to avoid or eliminate threats, loss, or pain will drive action. Therefore, when defining your question, recognize that pain often sells better than gain.

How to Use This Lens

In general, people will take greater risks to minimize (or reduce) pain or losses, yet are risk averse when the option is to increase their pleasure or gain. If your challenge implies a positive gain, ask:

- What is the pain we need to solve?
- What might be lost if we don't solve this problem?

Examples of This Lens in Action

In 1977, after investing hundreds of millions of dollars in automated teller machine (ATM) technology research and development, Citibank installed these machines across all of New York City (NYC). At first, the ATM was quite unpopular; people didn't see the benefit of a banking experience without tellers. A natural disaster turned that negativity around. In February 1978, a blizzard dumped nearly two feet of snow in NYC, bringing the city to a halt. The only place to get cash were the ATMs. It is estimated that during the storms, use of the machines increased by more than 20 percent, leading to their wildly popular slogan "The Citi Never Sleeps." By 1981, Citibank's market share of NYC deposits had doubled, largely due to the success of the ATM, which had been catapulted into popularity by the storm.

American psychologist Barry Schwartz once said that, "Appeals to women to do breast self-exams that emphasize the benefits of early cancer detection (gains) are less effective than those that emphasize the costs of late detection (losses)." Studies suggest that people are two or three times more likely to take action to prevent a loss than to achieve a gain.

Even telemarketers know that pain sells. Television infomercials always begin with the problem they solve, not with the solution. Tired of food spoiling too quickly? Buy this miracle bag-sealer system. Don't want to throw away those torn pants? Save them with this easy mending kit. No room in your closet? Use our clothes storage product that reduces the space needed.

#20: Bad Idea
Explore a Terrible Solution

Use This Lens When . . . You're Only
Looking at Good Solutions

Sometimes a way to crack the nut is to change the question and look for a terrible solution instead. This can be used as a starting point to find great solutions.

How to Use This Lens

You can engage this lens with two different strategies:

1. Instead of asking for great ideas, ask for terrible ones. Then ask "How can we turn this bad idea into a good one?" For example, think about the world prior to vaccines. What would be the dumbest way to prevent an outbreak of polio? Inject everyone with the virus. But, of course, that is exactly how it is done.
2. Instead of asking for what you want, ask what will give you what you don't want. Then do the opposite. For example, instead of increasing sales, find ways to decrease them and then do the opposite.

Examples of This Lens in Action

Consider a company whose manufacturing process is complex and potentially dangerous. The goal is to reduce accidents in the workplace. A good idea might be to add more safety inspectors. What would be a terrible idea? Firing all the safety inspectors. One company used this seemingly bad idea to develop a great one. Rather than having a few safety engineers scour the company for unsafe conditions, they transferred this responsibility to all of its employees, with rewards for both uncovering unsafe conditions and discovering new ways to conduct business more safely. This approach resulted in 35 to 50 percent improvements each year in the number and severity of accidents across the company.

America's flight to the moon was made possible through a terrible question: "What if the rocketship were to fall apart after takeoff?" Proposing the destruction of the rocketship sounds like a crazy idea. But this concept was a critical factor in the success of the Apollo missions: The rocket boosters containing the fuel fell off early during the trip to the moon, which allowed for the required lift and acceleration needed to exit the stratosphere.

 **zero-in on
an opportunity**

CHAPTER 9

Zero-In

When you are not sure if you are hitting the right target, these lenses will help you zero-in on the best direction. These lenses can (and should) be applied every time.

#21: Real Problem
Solve the Real Issue, Not the Symptoms

Use This Lens When . . . You Have Unexamined
Assumptions About Your Challenge

This is an important lens to use all the time. In fact, this should often be the first lens you use. When problem-solving, it is important that you are solving the real issue. Ask whether you are solving the right problem or whether you are just resolving the symptoms. No matter how efficiently you solve the wrong problem, the result will not matter.

How to Use This Lens

Ask:
- Do we really know the underlying problem we want to solve?
- Are we solving the root cause of the problem?

To ensure you are solving the right problem, you often need data [see the INSIGHTS lens (#23)]. When using this lens, it is useful to employ the assumption-busting tools described in chapter 3.

Examples of This Lens in Action

A consumer goods company invested a large amount of time and money trying to develop an alcohol-free mouthwash that was as effective as products containing alcohol, as they'd been told that's what customers wanted. "How can we create an alcohol-free mouthwash that is equally effective?" proved more difficult to solve for than they'd expected. Eventually, the product developers went back to the marketing department and discovered that, in fact, customers did not care if the mouthwash had alcohol, they just didn't like the *sting* associated with alcohol-based mouthwashes. The new challenge—"How can we create a mouthwash that doesn't sting?"—proved to be much easier to solve.

An office supply company asked the question "How can we more effectively sell our products to school administrators?" Their efforts to find solutions were irrelevant, because teachers were the real buyers; administrators merely filled out the paperwork. In this case, they should have done their homework to understand the real buyer before looking to find a solution.

An airline suffering high costs associated with their excess parts inventory assumed the problem was the result of their inventory-management processes. This assumption led to framing the problem around the question "How can we improve the inventory management process?" However, the real problem was that the airline used its own planes to move parts, viewing them as free transportation. As a result, spare parts often were left on the tarmac in order to make space for revenue-producing freight. The airline compensated for these self-imposed delays by keeping excess inventory on hand. Because of that, the best solution was found in framing the issue around the question "How can we improve the transportation of parts?" Asking the right question opened the range of solutions beyond simply streamlining warehouse operations.

#22: Real Business

Maybe You Are in a Different Industry Than You Think

Use This Lens When . . . You Have Unexamined Assumptions about Your Industry

It is always useful to make sure you are in the business you think you are in. Quite often, we make assumptions about our industry and competition. But with the blurring of industry boundaries, the explosion of tech start-ups and new entrants, and the introduction of game-changing technologies, it is important to make sure you think about your business in proper terms. All of these factors are changing the roles of companies and the competitors they need to fear. The risk in not using this lens is irrelevance.

How to Use This Lens

Ask:
- What business are we really in?
- Who are our real competitors?
- What new technology can make us irrelevant?

It is often useful to consider your industry in broader terms than you may be used to, and to consider competition that is outside your industry.

Examples of This Lens in Action

Although Marriott has traditionally been a hotel company, they now consider themselves to be a travel company. In April 2019, they introduced Homes & Villas by Marriott International. This moves them beyond hotels to houses, castles, and other luxury properties. This is a direct shot at their relatively new competitor, Airbnb. Marriott also recognizes that their competition isn't necessarily the other hotel chains but includes anyone who can own the guest relationship, including Online Travel Agencies (OTAs) such as Expedia and Google Travel. To proactively address this, Marriott penned a deal with Expedia in April 2019 designed to redefine their relationship from "competitor" to a "technology solutions provider."

Sometimes technology can force you to reevaluate your industry. UPS is known for moving physical goods from one location to another using trucks and planes, so its investment in self-driving vehicles makes perfect sense. However, a potentially more disruptive technology could impact them in the future: 3D printing. This technology allows products to be moved digitally, rather than physically, eliminating the need for trucks and planes. Knowing this, UPS has launched an "On-Demand 3D Printing Manufacturing Network" designed to get ahead of the game while adding 3D printing capabilities to many of their stores. Their real business has shifted from just trucks and planes to other forms of delivery.

#23: Insights
Identify Required Information

Use This Lens When . . . Additional Information
Would Be Helpful

This lens is useful in almost every situation. More data typically
will help you make better decisions. Although data is not
always available and has inherent limitations, if you have it—and
use it wisely—you often can find either root causes or opportunities. This lens is particularly useful when the challenge statement
seems vague, when you aren't sure if you are solving the REAL
PROBLEM (lens #21), or if you can't find the LEVERAGE point
(lens #1).

How to Use This Lens

Ask:
- Is there data that can give us insights into a
  better solution?
- Have we looked at the data to help us identify more
  specific areas of focus?
- What information would help reframe the question
  or even help find solutions?

Examples of This Lens in Action

A mobile phone operator suddenly experienced a surge of
calls into its call center. The company originally posed the question "How can we more effectively handle the increased volume of
customer calls?" This led to a wide range of ideas, none of which

proved to be effective. The volume was just too much. When they looked at the data for patterns, they discovered that there were a few lines on invoices that led to confusion and prompted additional calls. This led to the question "How can we make the invoice more intuitive?" When the company made changes to the bills, the number of calls instantly dropped. It wasn't a call center problem; it was a billing problem.

A financial services company wanted to solve the challenge "How can we offer services to our customers that they are currently buying from our competition?" They first asked their employees for ideas, but received only low-value suggestions. They realized that they needed more data, and so turned to their billions of dollars of customer credit card charges. When analyzed, they discovered that this information could help them determine which categories of services their customers were buying, leading them to high-value solutions.

#24: Variations
Avoid One-Size-Fits-All Approaches

Use This Lens When . . . Your Question Implies That
All Customers or Situations Can Be Treated the Same

Aone-size-fits-all challenge tends to be ineffective; consider
how you might address exceptions or rare cases in different
ways. But don't design around the most complicated or unlikely
cases. When designers try to create a standardized process that
covers every situation, no matter how rare or unusual, the result
is usually greatly increased complexity and diminishing returns.
Exceptions do not need to be treated the same or as efficiently.
Create variations in the way you do your work.

How to Use This Lens

Ask:
- How can we design a solution to handle the exception, not for the exception?
- How can we create multiple variations that serve different needs differently?

Examples of This Lens in Action

This is the approach taken by medical professionals, who
use different processes to handle different kinds of cases: out-
patient care for minor conditions such as flu; hospitalization
for major medical problems; and emergency care for urgent,
life-threatening situations.

A major life insurance company implicitly believed that

they should "process all claims equally and rigorously." As a result, every claim was being processed using the same time-consuming, expensive procedures. Knowing they needed to improve speed and cost, the company investigated treating exceptions differently from all standard claims. They asked the question "How can we treat most claims quickly and only handle exceptions with the rigorous process?" The result was a scaled and segmented claims process. For straightforward cases, a stream-lined process was used. More robust versions were used for more complicated cases, while the full process was reserved for only the most difficult and time-consuming cases. What they found was that 60 percent of cases could be handled using the simplest process with the least expensive resources. The result? Processing costs were reduced by 40 percent, while average processing time was greatly reduced and service levels improved.

#25: Observation
Uncover Hidden and Unarticulated Needs

Use This Lens When . . . Historical Data Isn't Enough

The traditional approach to gaining new insights into a problem space involves accumulating and analyzing data. But there are limitations in the value of data, as it tends to provide only an historical view of behavior. We typically have data only about current customers, not on future customers with future needs. And we only have information about their interaction with us as a company, not how they behave in their daily lives. In order to determine if you are asking the right questions, consider observing them to uncover hidden and unarticulated needs.

How to Use This Lens

Ask:
* Instead of asking our customers what they want, how can we observe them?

The concept of ethnography is one way to observe your customers. Instead of asking customers for their opinions via customer surveys or analyzing gigabytes of data, get out and watch them in action. Visit them in their homes. Watch them use your products. Create a lab where you can watch people in a controlled environment. The key is to avoid interfering with their activities. As much as possible, you want to observe them in their natural habitats.

Examples of This Lens in Action

Whirlpool developed pedestals and storage units for its Duet front-loading washers and dryers after visiting a customer's home and observing that she'd placed her dryer upon cinderblocks to make it easier to load and unload without having to bend over. In addition, the drawers that slide out from the pedestals provide an out-of-the-way space to store bottles of laundry detergent, bleach, and fabric softener. Had Whirlpool not observed this customer in action, the company might never have uncovered this hidden need.

Sometimes observation can even lead to a new business opportunity. Two entrepreneurs separately observed the difficulties people had with taking their medication. One saw how difficult it was for his father to keep track of his medicines after having surgery. The other delivered prescriptions as a teenager and observed how difficult it was for patients to deal with multiple medications. From these observations, in 2012, PillPack was born. This online service sorts and packages all of a patient's pills by date and time. In 2018, they were acquired by Amazon for nearly $1 billion.

CHALLENGE-CENTERED INNOVATION

66

We strive for quantity of ideas when, in fact, we really should be striving for quality of questions. Quantity drives waste; quality drives value.

CHAPTER 10

Leveraging Challenges for Innovation

This section is for leaders who are interested in using innovation as a way of growing their business and staying relevant. It provides perspectives and tools specifically for innovation to help you use the concepts you've read in this book.

It is important to note that this is a high-level perspective—we're only going to scratch the surface of what is needed to make innovation a reality. If you want to explore further, visit the Going Deeper section of this book, where I share other ways to learn more about the world of innovation and collaboration.

In this section, we will explore how to leverage questions (aka challenges) to drive a culture of innovation. We'll first look at the inefficient approaches used by many companies, then at an alternative approach called Challenge-Centered Innovation. Finally, I'll introduce you to my FAST Innovation model, an approach for increasing innovation ROI tenfold over traditional methods.

Asking for Ideas Is a Bad Idea

"Why did our innovation efforts fail so badly?"

It's a question many companies are asking themselves today, at the height of the innovation hype, when so much work has failed to generate the desired ROI.

I was asked it once again by a major European bank that brought me in to conduct a postmortem of their digital suggestion box initiative. They'd been looking to reinvigorate the business through innovation. Everything they'd done had actually resulted in the opposite: Instead of growing the business and engaging employees, the bank had wasted a lot of energy and ticked off the people who worked for them.

What went wrong?

The bank's employees had submitted ideas about how to improve the business to the digital suggestion box in droves. Unfortunately, of more than fifteen hundred submissions, only two were considered valuable enough to be implemented. Hundreds of employees took time from their busy schedules to submit their ideas, yet almost none of those ideas were put into action. No wonder the innovation program negatively affected morale. The bank shut down the program and fired the entire innovation team.

This situation is common. I've seen hundreds of companies get similar, less-than-stellar results with the suggestion box. What can we learn from them?

First and foremost, asking for ideas is a bad idea. Everyone has an opinion, suggestion, or idea—but that doesn't mean they're any good.

On March 19, 2008, Starbucks launched a collaborative website called "My Starbucks Idea." The goal was to get customers to submit their ideas about how to improve Starbucks. In late 2012, they released an infographic indicating that, during the first five years of this initiative, 150,000 ideas were submitted, but only 277 were implemented. Fewer than 0.2 percent of the ideas saw the light of day. Before retiring the site in 2017, Starbucks had received approximately 400,000 ideas and implemented about 800 of them.

Of course, this is great on some level. Eight hundred new ideas were implemented; that's nearly a hundred innovations per year! But think about the 399,200 other ideas that were not implemented. People took time out of their busy days to suggest various innovations—like a spinach-flavored latte—that Starbucks did nothing with. Is that good for the morale of the customers?

We strive for quantity of ideas when, in fact, we really should be striving for quality. Quantity drives waste; quality drives value.

One issue with asking for ideas is that it is difficult to find the good ones buried amongst the duds. It has been suggested that voting become a key part of the innovation process—but voting doesn't always lead to the desired result. For example, in 2016, the British government spent nearly $300 million building a polar research ship. They turned to the citizens of the United Kingdom to name the vessel, creating a polling platform that allowed people to submit and vote on their favorite name.

> Everyone has an opinion, suggestion, or idea—but that doesn't mean they're any good.

The winning name was *Boaty McBoatface*.

When hearing this story, people often assume that either 1) not a lot of people voted, or 2) the second most popular submission was close in the polls.

Incorrect. In the end, 124,000 people voted for *Boaty McBoatface*. The number two submission, *Poppy-Mai* (named after a girl who died from a fatal brain tumor and captured the hearts of the British), garnered just a small fraction at 34,000 votes.

Among my favorite submissions that landed in the Top 10:

- *It's Bloody Cold Here* was #4.
- For Olympic fans, you had *Usain Boat* coming in at #6.
- And, fans of American hip-hop music will love #10, *I Like Big Boats and I Cannot Lie*.

As it turns out, *Boaty McBoatface* was clever, but not wise. In the end, the government decided to use a different name for the boat, *David Attenborough* (#5), after the famous explorer.

Are crowds really wise?

As it turns out, many crowdsourcing initiatives, when they are done incorrectly, suffer from something called mobsourcing. This is when the vocal few crowd out the rest of the responses. Popular does not always equal best or correct.

Consider this the next time you ask people for their opinion or when you conduct customer surveys.

Idea-Driven Innovation

Let's deconstruct the traditional approach to innovation. The process starts with an idea. Any idea. It could be about a new or improved product, process, service, or business model. Regardless, innovation starts when someone is inspired.

Consider the life of an idea as a metaphorical funnel. At the top are all the ideas; at the bottom are the ones that make it through the evaluation process and on to implementation. That process involves four key steps: conception, submission, elimination, and selling.

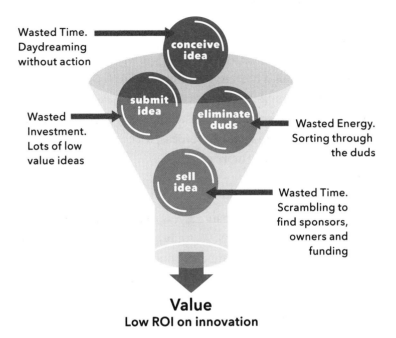

Wasted Time. Daydreaming without action → **conceive idea**

submit idea

eliminate duds

Wasted Investment. Lots of low value ideas →

← Wasted Energy. Sorting through the duds

sell idea

← Wasted Time. Scrambling to find sponsors, owners and funding

Value
Low ROI on innovation

Conceive an Idea

The entry point into the funnel is an idea. It's a rough idea. Just a concept. The creator thinks about it and tinkers with it for a while. Of course, most ideas are just ideas and nothing is ever done with them. The process of conceiving an idea takes time. Not a lot of time. But when we factor in the number of people in an organization who daydream about ideas, the aggregate amount of time is not insignificant. And, of course, only a small fraction of the ideas conceived ever get submitted.

Submit the Idea

We each believe some of our ideas have potential. Because we think these ideas will add value to the organization (and, in return, value to ourselves), we want to earn support for them. Maybe we submit them to suggestion boxes or tell someone in the organization who might help us move them forward.

Per idea, this process takes a lot more time than just conceiving one. Individuals need to position each idea so that it has perceived value and is easily understood by others. A fair amount of time has been invested by the time an idea is finally submitted. When a company encourages quantity of ideas, it ends up wasting a lot of that time—and hurting morale.

Eliminate the Duds

Next, we need to eliminate the less valuable ideas. This is when we evaluate the submissions. As we saw in the European bank and Starbucks examples, the number of submissions that get selected is abysmal. In most cases, less than 1 percent (more often closer to 0.1 percent) of submitted ideas are deemed valuable by evaluators. On average, at least 99 percent of the time spent thinking about the idea, submitting the idea, and evaluating the idea was a waste.

Why do we get so many bad suggestions? Recall the Goldilocks Principle we discussed in chapter 1: Suggestion boxes are merely vehicles for people to attempt to solve abstract questions (like "How can we improve the business?"), which invite a lot of random and typically low-value solutions.

Sell the Idea

At this point, we finally have some good ideas. Now we have the daunting task of selling those ideas internally, finding owners, sponsors, funding, and resources. Unfortunately, I have seen some excellent ideas that did not resonate with any business leaders, so the organizations passed on supporting the initiatives. Fortunately, some good ideas eventually do get the support they need, and the process of implementation begins.

At each step of the funnel, time and money are wasted. Given that most ideas are never submitted, time is wasted developing the raw concept. For those that are submitted, a minuscule fraction is deemed valuable. This wastes the time of the people who've submitted the rejected ideas, as well as the time of the evaluators who wade through the duds. Next, we lose more time trying to get support for the ideas that are deemed good. And all of this occurs before the real work even begins! This wasted work results in idea fatigue, which is when employees get tired of submitting ideas only to have them ignored or rejected. The idea-driven approach is inefficient. At the end of the day, you get a low ROI on your innovation efforts.

But that doesn't necessarily mean that there isn't value. Using this approach gets people engaged, which is important. They get used to the process, they get used to the tools, and they begin to feel more comfortable with innovation. Also, it results in some useful and potentially valuable submissions. (Not all of them. Probably only a small percentage of them. And most of them will be low-hanging fruit or ideas that have been considered in the past.)

Starting with ideas generates a low ROI and diverts energy from initiatives that could provide greater value. If your organization has an infinite amount of time, money, and resources, then the idea-driven approach might be right for you. But you don't! Time is precious. Budgets are being slashed and people are being asked to do more with less. Efficiency is the name of the game.

Fortunately, there is a better way.

Don't Think Outside the Box—Find a Better Box

If starting with ideas isn't the answer, where do we begin?

We start with questions. The question is an issue, problem, challenge, or opportunity that, if solved and implemented, will provide great value to the organization. And it needs to adhere to the Gold-ilocks principle.

I call this approach Challenge-Centered Innovation (CCI).

CCI consists of five steps: 1) define the differentiator and the challenge, 2) set the evaluation criteria, 3) identify and allocate resources, 4) look for solutions, and 5) experiment and execute. Let's look at these.

Define the Differentiator and the Challenge

CCI starts with a specific, well-defined, and differentiated challenge (see chapter 11, specifically the "Focus" part of the FAST Innovation model, for more on differentiation). The goal is to innovate where you differentiate. In other words, identify and solve the opportunities that help you stand out from the competition, because these opportunities are the ones that will add the most value.

In addition to choosing important challenges, we also must reframe them multiple times. It's that fifty-nine minutes spent defining the problem and one minute spent finding solutions that we discussed before. (This is the "Ask" step of the FAST Innovation process; see chapter 11).

Set the Evaluation Criteria

The next step is to set clear objective evaluation criteria that help with the selection process. With the traditional approach, the only way to evaluate an idea is against its own merits. If you are looking to solve a challenge, you know which attributes and qualities are desirable in the solution. By having clear and objective criteria, you know when you get a good solution and can objectively choose the best ones.

Identify and Allocate Resources

Another advantage of CCI is that you allocate the resources before investing in the solution. We get the money, people, sponsors, and owners upfront. This ensures that when you find a great solution, you can move forward immediately. Compare this to idea-driven innovation, where you scramble to get money, people, sponsors, and owners only after you find an idea you like.

This also is the time to choose evaluators who have a good understanding of the challenge and the bigger picture, ensuring that the needed support is lined up before any time is invested.

Look for Solutions

Once a differentiating challenge has been defined, the evaluation criteria have been set, and the resources have been allocated, it's time to look for solutions. Another advantage of identifying challenges over ideas is that when we look for solutions to our well-framed challenges, we don't get inundated with thousands of useless ideas like Starbucks or the European bank did. In addition, when done correctly, we can look outside our area of expertise for solutions. This will often accelerate the solution-finding process. (This is the "Shift" portion of the FAST Innovation Model; see chapter 11.)

Experiment and Execute

After solutions have been identified, it's time to move into implementation. It's important to start building small, scalable experiments that allow you to test your hypothesis. The goal of innovation is success, not failure. (This is the "Test" step of the FAST Innovation process; see chapter 11.)

Although you likely have been told to think outside the box in order to find creative solutions, the reality is that you want to find a better box. The better box is that well-framed challenge that drives high-value innovation.

Many of my clients have used the Challenge-Centered Innovation process, and the results have been staggering. One of my clients measures everything, including the ROI of its submitted and implemented ideas, the ROI on its challenges, and the time-to-market for everything. In the end, leadership consistently found that the organization got at least a tenfold increase in ROI when it focused on challenges rather than ideas. The speed of implementation was significantly faster because the organization eliminated the wasted energy in the process, and it was more likely to leverage a wider range of techniques for finding solutions. Applying my Challenge-Centered Innovation process to your organization can provide the same type of benefit.

> **"**
>
> *When you get everyone collaborating around well-framed challenges, you increase ROI, drive higher levels of efficiency, and reduce overall risk.*

CHAPTER 11

FAST Innovation

Now that we have established the power of Challenge-Centered Innovation, it's time to explore the four-step process.

1. Innovation starts with stating the issue, problem, challenge, or opportunity. It starts with the question, not the answer. Therefore, we must first make sure we are asking important questions—specifically, questions that will drive the greatest returns and create a sustainable competitive advantage. This is where we explore your differentiator.

2. Once we have established our priorities, it's time to identify specific challenges to solve. We've discussed the concept; now, in this chapter, we will dig deeper into the process.

3. When we've identified problems to solve and we have applied the lenses to reframe them, it is time to find solutions. Because our past experiences cloud our ability to see breakthrough solutions, we need to shift our perspectives and look elsewhere.

4. Finally, when we have a solution we want to implement, we need to conduct experiments that validate or refute the innovation.

These four steps are the backbone of the innovation work I've done with my clients for the past twenty years. This is the reverse-engineered process I referred to in the introduction. I started with the need for a highly efficient and highly effective method for innovation and eliminated any steps that weren't creating value. As a result, this streamlined process can help any organization create a culture of innovation without a lot of wasted time, money, or energy.

These four steps are neatly summarized in my **FAST** Innovation process:

Focus—Focus on differentiators
Ask—Ask better questions
Shift—Shift your perspective to find solutions
Test—Test, experiment, and implement solutions

FOCUS: Focus on Differentiators

There is a belief in the world of innovation that everyone should be innovating everywhere. Although engaging all your employees is indeed a great idea, innovating everywhere is a mistake.

Not all opportunities in your organization are equal. You can't solve every problem. If you try to be great at everything, you'll be great at nothing. Instead of trying to solve every problem, you want to innovate *only where you differentiate*. Focusing your energy on those activities and opportunities will have the greatest positive impact on your organization. Differentiating opportunities will help you stand out from the competition.

Identifying differentiators requires time and guidance. It is difficult to do on your own because of your blind spots. However, there is a useful framework that will help you get started: the 5Ds of Differentiation. All good differentiators include each of these five attributes:

1. **Distinct:** It sets you apart from the competition.
2. **Durable:** It is difficult for someone else to replicate.
3. **Disruption-Proof:** It will stand the test of time in a fast-changing world.
4. **Desirable:** People are willing to pay for it.
5. **Disseminated:** People inside and outside your organization are familiar with it.

> If you try to be great at everything, you'll be great at nothing.

Distinct

The key to being distinctive is to do something that sets you apart from the competition. This is the "different" in differentiation. It is why customers do business with you and not someone else.

Let's take a look at an example. Two insurance companies, State Farm and USAA, have distinctive strategies. State Farm's motto is "Like a good neighbor, State Farm is there." The company has the largest distribution network of independent branded agents. In an age when most companies have replaced the human touch with internet-based services, having a local, personal presence nearly everywhere has secured State Farm's position as the largest insurance company. They've captured 10 percent of the overall property and casualty market. They own 18 percent of the automotive insurance premiums and 21 percent of the home insurance market.

USAA, on the other hand, offers insurance and financial services only to those in the military and their families. The company's mantra is "Serve those who serve the country." With this focus, year after year, USAA has achieved a #1 or #2 customer service rating when measured against any company across all industries. Each year, USAA retains 98 percent of its members, and 92 percent say they will never leave.

State Farm's differentiator is the personal touch, which the company creates through its distribution network. USAA's differentiator is specialized service. Both companies invest heavily in these distinct differentiators.

Durable

You need to protect your differentiator. This could be done with legal structures like patents and trademarks, but more often, the key is to focus on differentiators that will be difficult for others to replicate.

I worked with a home assurance company that offers to fix appliances if they break. When I asked the leaders of the business "What is your differentiator?" everybody agreed it was their pricing models, which they believed to be unique. When I asked how soon the competition replicated any new pricing models they introduced, I was told that it happens, on average, within two weeks.

This is not a unique differentiator. And it is certainly not durable. This is you doing the hard work for your competition.

After further exploration, it was determined that the company's true differentiator was its extensive network of repairmen, which could not be recreated by a competitor. They reallocated their investments into nurturing this network.

Disruption-Proof

Companies and industries are being disrupted on a regular basis. New companies, emerging technologies, and shifting buyer behaviors can quickly render a company's business model irrelevant. To stand the test of time, you need to make sure your differentiator is disruption-proof.

To be clear, being disruption-proof does not mean your differentiator needs to change the rules of the game. You don't have to be disruptive in order to be disruption-proof. However, you do need a differentiator that's not going to become worthless in the future. For instance, the taxi industry long relied on its monopoly as the only paid hailed-ride service as its differentiator; once Uber launched, that monopoly was gone—and so was the taxi industry's competitive advantage. Similarly, Airbnb is changing the hotel industry, 3D printing is beginning to impact the supply chain, and blockchain is causing heartache and opportunity in financial services. Meanwhile, artificial intelligence (AI) is disrupting nearly every business in every industry.

The moral of the story is that what made you special in the past may no longer be sufficient.

Protecting your differentiator and being disruption-proof isn't just about today's competitors. You also need to worry about tomorrow's competitors. And it is not just technology that you need to worry about: Societal changes are affecting every industry. Tobacco companies, for example, are continually facing increased pressure from regulators. Soft drink manufacturers and fast food restaurants are being affected by the fight against obesity. Food manufacturers are seeing unhealthy ingredients negatively impact sales. To top it off, Millennials and GenZers are shifting generational consumer behavior. Your biggest competition might not necessarily be a nimble company or a new app—it could be economic and societal shifts that impact the buying decisions of your customers.

Desirable

Just because you *can* offer a new product or service to your customers doesn't mean you *should*: People need to be willing to pay for your differentiators.

In Atlantic City, the Revel was built in 2012 for over $2.5 billion. It's a spectacular, sophisticated, and classy high-end casino. There's only one problem: The people who go to Atlantic City typically are not looking for spectacular, sophisticated, classy, or high-end experiences. People go to Atlantic City to enjoy the beach with their kids, eat cotton candy and hotdogs, and maybe play nickel slots. In 2014, the Revel went bankrupt and shut its doors. Neither its design nor its product were desirable to the people who visit Atlantic City.

Being different is not the same as being differentiated. What makes you distinct and different also must be desirable. Your customers must value what you offer.

Disseminated

Finally, for something to truly be a differentiator, people need to know about it, both internally and externally. At the end of the day, although you can declare your differentiator, the market ultimately will determine the value of it with their wallets. When you ask customers "Why do you do business with us and not the competition?" they should be able to articulate the differentiator you are focused on. Therefore, it is critical that you share your differentiator externally. It is equally important that you share your differentiator internally, because it sets the direction for the company and serves as a compass, ensuring that everyone is solving the same problem—and a problem that is valuable to the organization. It is a great way to prioritize your innovation investments.

One company that has done this particularly well is Westin. I've worked with hotels for many years, and when I would ask people on the street "Which hotel chain has the best beds?" most people would tell me Westin. Why? Because Westin has branded the Heavenly Bed, and they have done a great job of getting that message out to the world. Make sure your company's differentiator is not a best kept secret.

ASK: Ask Better Questions

Once you are clear about your differentiator, the next step in the FAST Innovation process is to ask better questions that drive higher-value results. A company has challenges everywhere—the key is uncovering them. This is especially true of the hidden (aka assumption-based) challenges that can put you out of business. There are several ways you can find them.

Ask Executives to Name Challenges

This actually is where I like to start: Identify the people who have the money and the power in the company. But don't go to them talking about innovation, since that word activates antibodies that make people want to run in the other direction. Instead, ask them to name their three most pressing challenges. Ask them what keeps them up at night. If it is important to them, it is important to you.

Once you know their three most pressing challenges, offer to help find solutions. Executives typically are more open to this type of support than if you say, "Hey, I'm going to come in and help you innovate." Get this list of challenges from top executives, business unit leads, lines of business heads, and P&L owners—basically from anyone with power and money. This is a starter list of challenges. Although not all the items will be great, this is a wonderful way to get early buy-in from top leaders into the process of problem-solving. This buy-in can help you gain momentum for longer-term success. Besides, you will have gotten your sponsors and funding in place for the challenges up-front.

Go External to Identify Challenges

Even the smartest people within the best organizations have blind spots. They are too close to the business and therefore have reduced peripheral vision. That's why it is useful to partner with external groups, like trend-monitoring organizations, universities, think tanks, consultants, and other experts, to help identify the challenges that might fall in the organization's blind spots.

Think tanks and trend watchers can help you look to the future and forecast what shifts (technological, economic, societal, etc.) could affect your business. You also can get some amazing insights from customers, partners, vendors, and suppliers. In fact, one of my clients set up an entire innovation program around vendors, because they knew they would have insights into new opportunities that were in their development pipelines.

Ask Employees to Identify Challenges

If we rely only on leaders for their input, we create a highly undesirable top-down approach to innovation. We want to tap into the insights of everyone inside the organization, so we need to get employees involved in the process of identifying challenges.

Instead of the "Don't bring me problems, bring me solutions" mantra, teach employees to find bigger, more important, and better-framed challenges. You want to strive for quality, not quantity. This step requires education and guidance to avoid being inundated by poorly defined or low-value challenges. It is imperative that people submit challenges and not ideas masquerading as challenges. You need to give them the tools to become better at reframing issues so that they do this work, rather than having to delegate it to a small, core team. The key is to make sure that you don't create another useless suggestion box.

If you ask employees to submit their challenges, recognize that some people may need additional incentives to participate. Incentives could take myriad forms.

For example, researchers set up a competition at University of California San Diego's Jacobs School of Engineering. Some students wanted to participate simply because it sounded interesting.

But a number of students did not initially respond to the participation request, so they were offered a financial reward for participating. Although conventional wisdom would lead us to believe that those who were intrinsically motivated would perform best, research showed that those who were financially persuaded were just as capable. Their success was statistically indistinguishable from those who were innately drawn to the competition. Why? Because some people don't participate because they don't consider themselves to be innovative. Don't assume everyone is naturally inclined to contribute—some people need a little push.

There are many other places to look for your challenges, including using the assumption-busting techniques mentioned in chapter 3.

SHIFT: Shift Your Perspective

Once you have well-framed and differentiating challenges, it is time to find solutions. This is the "Shift" part of the FAST Innovation model. As you will see, sometimes simply changing the question is the fastest way to shift your perspective and find a better solution.

When solving complex problems, our expertise limits the range of solutions we might consider. The more we know about a topic, the more difficult it is for us to think differently about it. Our answers, just like our questions, are often based on past experience. This isn't necessarily bad, but it tends to lead to incremental innovation. In some cases, it might even prevent finding workable solutions. Compound this with the fact that smart people are often more interested in being right rather than doing what is right, and you end up with a limited range of options. To shift your perspective, you need to bring together people from a wide range of disciplines, backgrounds, and experiences.

Who Else Has Solved a Similar Problem?

One of the most effective ways I have found to quickly solve a challenge is to ask a simple question: "Who else …?"—e.g., "Who else has solved a similar problem?" Not the same problem, but a similar problem in a different domain space. [This concept was explored in the ANALOGY lens (#6).]

> The more we know about a topic, the more difficult it is for us to think differently about it.

One of my favorite examples comes from a potato chip manufacturer that wanted to create a low-fat chip that tasted like the full-fat version. Basically, the company wanted to make a full-fat potato chip, then shake off as much of the fat as possible. To see if it could do this, the company cooked the potatoes in a deep fat fryer, then put the chips on a vibrating conveyor belt that caused the fat to drip off. By the time the chips got to the end of the conveyor belt, the company had low-fat potato chips! One problem: The chips had turned into crumbs.

Without a better solution, the manufacturer asked a "who else?" question: "Who else vibrates something fragile without breaking it?"

When I ask audiences this question, most people assume the answer came from the egg industry, because they're looking for solutions as close as possible to the potato chip industry.

In this case, the solution did not come from the food industry at all—it was provided by a musician, who noticed that when he played his bass, a fragile glass would vibrate, but it wouldn't break. Armed with this experience, he went home, cooked up some potato chips, put them on a drying rack, and placed a loud speaker over it. He tinkered with the frequency and volume until he got the potato chips to dance, shaking off the fat without them breaking. Sound is now one of the techniques used to blast the fat off potato chips. Going from music to potato chips is quite a shift—and it works.

Purposeful Tangents

Another great example comes from an annual event called Pumps and Pipes. A group of cardiologists get together with people from the oil/gas pipeline industry and share what they know about the cardio-vascular system and how it could apply to the transmission of oil/gas, and *vice versa*. What these two industries share in common is that they both solve problems around fluids moving through tubes.

I call Pumps and Pipes a purposeful tangent: purposefully choosing to spend time with others who are tangential to your world. The solutions that can come from collaborations like this are amazing. For example, filters in pipelines are used to reduce sludge in oil fields. Adapting this solution, cardiologists built a device to filter blood clots (essentially sludge in the veins) from the venous system. The result is the Greenfield inferior vena cava filter, a major breakthrough in reducing pulmonary embolisms.

Think about where you spend your professional development time. If you are like most people, nearly 100 percent of your time is spent learning from people in your own industry or function. Solutions are everywhere—not just within your company or your industry. The key is to know how to find the best solutions with the least amount of effort. To gather new perspectives, I encourage you to spend a percentage of your time connecting with people from different industries or functions. Not random ones, but ones that are adjacent to yours. For example, one of my purposeful tangents is magic. Magicians spend their lives trying to make the impossible possible. This is something innovators would love to be able to do.

As I like to say, rocket science isn't always rocket science. If you have a hundred rocket scientists trying to solve an aerospace problem and you still can't find a solution, adding one more rocket scientist to the mix probably will not make a shred of difference. But looking to other industries—like lingerie and Hollywood—can lead to better solutions. NASA developed solutions to one of its problems by studying the gossamer properties of lingerie, and air bags used by stuntmen were adapted to create a soft landing for spacecraft.

Although it is beyond the scope of this book, open innovation and crowdsourcing, when done right, are fantastic tools for shifting perspectives and finding breakthrough solutions.

If expertise is the enemy of breakthrough innovation, it's time to shift your perspective and connect with people from other industries and disciplines.

TEST: Test, Experiment, and Implement Solutions

Once we find solutions to our pressing challenges, it's time to move forward with implementation. This is the "Test" portion of the FAST Innovation Model.

The concept of failure is now in vogue. It seems as though everyone is being told that in order to increase their level of innovation, they must fail more quickly and more often. Although failure might be the inevitable outcome of innovation, it should not be the goal. We don't want to strive for failure. Instead, we want to become masters of experimentation so that we can minimize the risk.

One of the primary causes of failure might surprise you.

We typically joke that "yeah, but" is the enemy of innovation. We've all been told that we need to stop uttering those words and replace them with "yes, and . . ." But what if "yeah, but" is not the problem? What if there is something more insidious and less obvious?

A bigger enemy of innovation is "Wow, this is a great idea."

You read that correctly. Falling in love with your own ideas is the surest way for them to fail. The main reason for this is something we discussed earlier: confirmation bias, when the brain filters information and provides only the data that supports your beliefs, rejecting everything else.

We see confirmation bias in all areas of life. Our view of politicians and politics is driven by it. Your purchasing decisions are influenced by it. If you really want a particular car, for example, no number of bad reviews will change your mind. You will look at the positive ones and justify why the negative ones are wrong.

This happens in innovation, too. When conducting experiments, if you believe your idea is great, you will only find evidence that supports that belief. You will either reject or justify conflicting evidence.

Loving your ideas creates confirmation bias. It also leads to another fatal error: positive test strategy. This happens when you run experiments designed only to prove that your ideas are good, forgetting to conduct experiments designed specifically to show that they might, in fact, be stinkers.

When you combine these two together—i.e., confirmation bias and positive test strategy—you end up with a recipe for disaster. You continue investing in ideas that should be killed.

How do you prevent this?

The first step is to recognize that this is the way we are wired as human beings. Studies show that simply being aware of confirmation bias can reduce its impact. For example, researchers gave trained U.S. Army intelligence analysts a battlefield scenario. After forming an initial hypothesis, the analysts were given updated intelligence reports. Even though these reports contained significant evidence that disproved their beliefs, the analysts held fast to their initial hypotheses and, in fact, increased their confidence levels.

Researchers ran the test again with the same participants, but before doing so, they showed participants how confirmation bias negatively impacted their decision making the first time around. During the second trial, the participants were given visual reminders designed to help foster their awareness of alternative hypotheses.

The result was a "lower level of confidence, greater consideration of alternative enemy courses of action, and more willingness to reverse early decisions based on new evidence." In fact, during the second trial, 50 percent of the participating teams changed their hypothesis at least once during the exercise.

But being aware of confirmation bias is not enough to eliminate it. For extra protection, make sure that the individuals testing the idea are not the same as those who developed it in the first place. In addition, I find it helpful to have a devil's advocate team. Their job is to uncover all the reasons that an innovation should be killed. They neutralize the positive test strategy issue by conducting experiments specifically designed to disprove the hypothesis.

Scott Cook, the founder of Intuit, once said, "For every one of our failures we had spreadsheets that looked awesome." This is brilliant! We can make any idea seem like a great idea. But the key to winning with innovation is to know which bets to place and which to avoid.

Killing innovation is a normal part of the innovation process. Knowing where to invest and where not to invest is critical.

Of course, implementation does not end with experimentation. It is the first step. And it is a crucial step.

<hr>

With Challenge-Centered Innovation and the FAST Innovation process, you now have the tools to start creating a high-performing innovation culture. When you get everyone collaborating around well-framed challenges, you increase ROI, drive higher levels of efficiency, and reduce overall risk. The next step is to take the concepts from this book and apply them to your organization.

Fortunately, innovation and problem-solving are not just for the right-brained creative types. Anyone can participate. We are all innovative; we just innovate in different ways. When you view innovation as a process that starts with a challenge and ends with the creation of value, even left-brained nerds can be major contributors to a company's innovation efforts.

Walt Disney once said, "It's kind of fun to do the impossible." I, like many others, love a good challenge. But the effort does not need to seem Herculean.

Learn the tools provided in this book. Memorize them. Use them, again and again, until they are inextricably linked with the DNA of your innovation process. I promise that you'll quickly move from the seemingly impossible to the possible, and ultimately, to the probable.

Closing Thoughts

The summer after my freshman year of college, I worked in maintenance in a warehouse that shipped shoes. It was hot as hell inside that building. I had the fun tasks of oiling conveyor belts, cleaning windows, and sweeping the floors (amongst other things).

I vividly recall sweeping one day—brushing the dirt onto a shovel, walking ten feet to the trash can, then walking back to resume my sweeping. The next time I had the shovel full, I was twelve feet away from the trash can, sweating and tired. I went back and forth a dozen times while my supervisor watched, shaking his head. Eventually he came up to me and said, "Move the trash can closer to where you are sweeping, and you'll save a lot of time and energy."

To most people, this is probably an obvious solution. But while I was in the middle of the job, my brain never considered the option.

As silly as this example may seem, it is a great illustration of what occurs on a daily basis in most organizations. You are an expert. You know your job. You know your function. You know your company. You know your industry. But sometimes that means you are too close to the problem. Just as I never thought to move the trash can, most people, when solving problems, never think to move the question.

But, as we have established, the key to finding better solutions is to look at the problem with different eyes. We need to shine a light on our blind spots. We need to bring our assumptions to the surface. And we need to use tools (e.g., the lenses) in order to help us see opportunities—especially the ones that are right in front of us.

Have fun playing with the lenses. See how many different ways you can reframe the question—turn it into a game. Get your teammates involved. Have a competition to see who can come up with the most outrageous question. Even though you are building a mental muscle, it doesn't have to be work.

Going Deeper

This book provides a high-level perspective on what is needed to make innovation work in an organization. If you are interested in more information, I have a few resources that will help you dig deeper.

The first place to start is my previous book, *Best Practices Are Stupid: 40 Ways to Out-Innovate the Competition* (Portfolio Penguin, 2011). That book addresses a wider range of topics, including motivation strategies, measures, organization structures, crowdsourcing, market research and more. (See www.stupidpractices.com.)

If you are interested in creating high-performing innovation teams, I strongly urge you to learn about my Personality Poker® system. This fun yet powerful card game will help you better understand how everyone on your team can most effectively contribute to your innovation efforts. (See www.personalitypoker.com.)

If you want to dig really deep, check out my Innovation Intervention program. This is an eight-week, hands-on, guided, intensive look into all aspects of innovation. It includes videos, templates, downloads, deliverables, group calls, one-on-one calls, and email support. (See www.innovationintervention.com.)

And if you really want to dig even deeper, contact me directly. We can explore how my training programs, speeches, workshops, and advisory services could help you with your innovation and problem-solving efforts. Write me at solutions@StephenShapiro.com or visit us at www.StephenShapiro.com.

SUPPORTING RESOURCES, NOTES, AND ACKNOWLEDGMENTS

Supporting Resources

Here are some tools to help you through the process, answer a few questions, and ask much stronger ones.

The **Lenses Cheat Sheet** is the fold-out in the hardcover version of the book. You can download a printable copy, along with the **Challenge Template**, at www.invisiblesolutionsresources.com.

There, you'll also find links to a variety of software and multimedia we've developed to help you maximize the results you get from the book. We are currently experimenting with **mobile and web software, chat bots,** and **video** that will enable you to quickly get up to speed with the material, dive deeply into the lenses and their application, and uncover optimal solutions!

To access **HYPONYMS** and **HYPERNYMS** (lenses #5 and #10, respectively) at a glance, use the following resources:

- http://wordnetweb.princeton.edu/perl/webwn (Click "S"; in some cases, hyponyms are listed as troponyms)
- http://conceptnet.io (More user-friendly site that does not use the terms hypernym or hyponym)

If you want to learn more about **viscous shearing**, watch

this great video by my colleague Steve Spangler: https://youtu.be/
RUMX_b_m3Js.

You can find a good overview of Harvard's **Implicit Association
Test** on Wikipedia: https://en.wikipedia.org/wiki/Implicitassociation
_test. To take a test, go to https://implicit.harvard.edu/implicit/.

Notes

Front Matter

Twain, Mark, and Michael J. Kiskis (editor). 2010. *Mark Twain's Own Autobiography: The Chapters from the North American Review*. 2nd ed. Madison: University of Wisconsin Press.

Chapter 1

Lech, Robert K., Onur Güntürkün, and Boris Suchan. 2016. "An Interplay of Fusiform Gyrus and Hippocampus Enables Prototype- and Exemplar-Based Category Learning." *Behavioural Brain Research* 311: 239-246. https://doi.org/10.1016/j.bbr.2016.05.049.

Schmit, Julie. 2010. "After BP Oil Spill, Thousands of Ideas Poured in for Cleanup." *USA Today*, November 15, 2010. http://www.usatoday.com/money/industries/environment/2010-11-15-gulfcleanup15_CV_N.htm.

Einstein, Albert, and Leopold Infeld. 1967. *The Evolution of Physics*. 18th
ed. New York City: Touchstone Books. [Note: It is unclear if Einstein
ever said these exact words, but a variation can be properly attributed
to this 1938 quote: "The mere formulation of a problem is far more
often essential than its solution, which may be merely a matter of
mathematical or experimental skill. To raise new questions, new
possibilities, to regard old problems from a new angle requires creative
imagination and marks real advances in science."]

Kelleher, Kevin. 2018. "The Rise and Fall of Sears: A Timeline from Its
Founding to Its Bankruptcy." *Fortune*, October 15, 2018. https://fortune.
com/2018/10/15/the-rise-and-fall-of-sears-a-timeline-from-its-founding-
to-its-bankruptcy/.

Sweeney, Brigid. 2012. "Where America Shopped." *Crain's Chicago Business*,
April 21, 2012. https://www.chicagobusiness.com/article/20120421/
ISSUE01/304219970/special-report-sears-where-america-shopped.

Katz, Donald. 1987. *The Big Store: Inside the Crisis and Revolution at Sears*. New
York: Viking.

Desjardins, Jeff. 2018. "10 Skills You'll Need to Survive the Rise of
Automation." The World Economic Forum, July 2, 2018. https://www.
weforum.org/agenda/2018/07/the-skills-needed-to-survive-the-robot-
invasion-of-the-workplace.

Lewis, Gregory. 2019. "The Most In-Demand Hard and Soft Skills of 2019."
LinkedIn Talent Blog, January 3, 2019. https://business.linkedin.com/
talent-solutions/blog/trends-and-research/2018/the-most-in-demand-
hard-and-soft-skills-of-2018.

Mueller, Jennifer S., Shimul Melwani, and Jack A. Goncalo. 2010. "The Bias
Against Creativity: Why People Desire but Reject Creative Ideas." Ithaca:
Cornell University ILR School. https://digitalcommons.ilr.cornell.edu/
articles/450/.

Chapter 2

Shafir, Eldar. 1993. "Choosing Versus Rejecting: Why Some Options are Both Better and Worse Than Others." *Memory & Cognition* 21 (4): 546-556. https://link.springer.com/content/pdf/10.3758%2FBF03197186.pdf

Parker-Pope, Tara. 2000. "Weapons Against Dust Mites May Not Be Worth the Cost." *The Wall Street Journal*, February 18, 2000. https://www.wsj.com/articles/SB950819617226695844.

Chapter 3

Estrin, James. 2015. "Kodak's First Digital Moment." *The New York Times*, August 12, 2015. https://lens.blogs.nytimes.com/2015/08/12/kodaks-first-digital-moment/?_r=0.

Kuzmanovic, Bojana, Lionel Rigoux, and Marc Tittgemeyer. 2018. "Influence of vmPFC on dmPFC Predicts Valence-Guided Belief Formation." *The Journal of Neuroscience* 38 (37): 7996-8010. https://doi.org/10.1523/JNEUROSCI.0266-18.2018.

Chapter 5

Takahashi, Dean. 2019. "SuperData: Digital Games Grew 13% to $119.6 Billion in 2018; Fortnite earned $2.4 Billion." *VentureBeat*, January 16, 2019. https://venturebeat.com/2019/01/16/superdata-digital-games-grow-12-to-109-8-billion-in-2018-fortnite-earned-2-4-billion/.

Chapter 7

Walmart, Inc. (WMT). UBS Global Consumer & Retail Conference (transcript), March 6, 2019. https://corporate.walmart.com/media-library/document/2019-ubs-global-consumer-retail-conference-webcast-transcript/_proxyDocument?id=00000169-7873-d4ef-adeb-7b73b8e00000.

Chapter 8

Schwartz, Barry. 2007. "When Words Decide." *Scientific American Mind*, August 2007. https://www.scientificamerican.com/article/when-words-decide/.

Kahneman, Daniel, and Amos Tversky. 2000. "1983 APA Awards Addresses." *Choices, Values, and Frames*. Cambridge: Cambridge University Press.

Florian, Ellen. 2004. "The Money Machines." *Fortune*, July 26, 2004. https://money.cnn.com/magazines/fortune/fortune_archive/2004/07/26/377172/.

Chapter 9

Glusac, Elaine. 2019. "A New Marriott Division Goes Head-to-Head with Airbnb." *The New York Times*, April 29, 2019. https://www.nytimes.com/2019/04/29/travel/marriott-airbnb-homeshare-luxury.html.

Ting, Deanna. 2019. "Marriott's New Contract with Expedia Signals a Shift in the Direct Booking Wars." *Skift*, April 11, 2019. https://skift.com/2019/04/11/marriotts-new-contract-with-expedia-signals-a-shift-in-the-direct-booking-wars/.

United Parcel Service of America, Inc. 2016. "UPS to Launch On-Demand 3D Printing Manufacturing Network." UPS Pressroom, May 18, 2016. https://pressroom.ups.com/pressroom/ContentDetailsViewer.page?ConceptType=PressReleases&id=1463510444185-310.

Munarriz, Rick. 2008. "Blockbuster CEO Has Answers." *The Motley Fool*, December 10, 2008. https://www.fool.com/investing/general/2008/12/10/blockbuster-ceo-has-answers.aspx.

Verhage, Julie, and Robert Langreth. 2018. "Amazon's PillPack Acquisition All Started with an MIT Hackathon." *Bloomberg*, June 28, 2018. https://www.bloomberg.com/news/articles/2018-06-28/amazon-s-pillpack-acquisition-all-started-with-an-mit-hackathon.

Chapter 10

Hale, Tom. 2016. "'Boaty McBoatface' Just Won the Antarctic Ship Name Vote." *IFLScience!*, April 18, 2016. https://www.iflscience.com/environment/boaty-mcboatface-winner-antarctic-ship-name-vote-dont-get-your-hopes/

Chapter 11

"The Largest Home Insurance Companies by Market Share." *Insure*, August 1, 2012. https://www.insure.com/home-insurance/largest-home-insurance-companies-by-market-share.html.

"2016 Market Share Reports." *National Association of Insurance Commissioners*, 2017. https://www.naic.org/prod_serv/MSR-PB-17.pdf.

Adriano, Lyle. 2018. "Allstate Loses Top Three Spot for Auto Insurance Market Share." *Insurance Business Magazine*, April 4, 2018. https://www.insurancebusinessmag.com/us/news/breaking-news/allstate-loses-top-three-spot-for-auto-insurance-market-share-96841.aspx.

Foxman, Simone, and Christopher Palmeri. 2018. "Atlantic City's Failed $2.6 Billion Casino Rolls the Dice." *Bloomberg,* June 22, 2018. https://www.bloomberg.com/news/articles/2018-06-22/atlantic-city-s-failed-2-6-billion-casino-rolls-the-dice.

Clark, Christine. 2018. University of California – San Diego. "Anyone Can Be an Innovator: Students Given Incentives to Innovate are Just as Skilled as the Self-Motivated." *ScienceDaily,* April 19, 2018. https://www.sciencedaily.com/releases/2018/04/180419100151.htm.

Tolcott, Martin A., and F. Freeman Marvin. 1995. United States Army Research Institute for the Behavioral and Social Sciences. "Reducing the Confirmation Bias in an Evolving Situation." *ARI Research Note 95-27*, February 1995. https://apps.dtic.mil/dtic/tr/fulltext/u2/a293570.pdf.

McGregor, Jena. "How Failure Breeds Success." *Businessweek,* July 10, 2006. https://www.bloomberg.com/news/articles/2006-07-09/how-failure-breeds-success.

Some of the content in this book previously appeared in articles I published on Inc.com. You can see all of those articles, and more, at: https://www.inc.com/author/stephen-shapiro.

Acknowledgments

For me, writing the acknowledgments is always the most difficult part. Over the years, so many people have shared concepts, comments, and content that ultimately made their way into my books. It would be impossible to thank everyone who has contributed, but I do want to recognize a few people.

First and foremost, I want to thank my wife, Elénie. Her support and wisdom have made me a better person. She has opened my eyes in so many positive ways and has helped me grow as a husband, business person, and human being. Words could never express the deep appreciation I have for her, her guidance, and her love.

I want to thank my awesome sister, Deborah, who has been a rock star in my business for more than a decade, keeping everything running smoothly. And, as always, I am eternally grateful to my parents for their love and support.

A special thank you to Adam Leffert. The day I mentioned I was going to write another book, he was on the phone with me, providing direction throughout the entire process. He was the one who suggested *Invisible Solutions* for the title. Plus, he helped provide valuable feedback on the cover, subtitle, layout, content, and nearly every aspect of the book. Not only was he an incredible sounding board during the development of the book, he is the technical guru who is creating all of the supporting software (e.g., mobile and web apps, chat bots, videos, etc.). If you ever need software developed, I strongly encourage you to learn more about him at www.fullstackdeveloper.com.

This super cool and unusual cover was the brainchild of John Brunswick. In addition to being an innovation and technology leader at a major software company, he is also ridiculously creative. He created the first iteration of the book cover you see here. The invisible man, the reflective glasses, the subtle words on the jacket, and the purple background were all his idea. The second I saw it, I knew we had a winner. And the distinctive coloration has been carried throughout the entire book.

Thank you, Clint Greenleaf, for all of your support throughout the entire process. Your knowledge of the book industry is extraordinary.

Although literally hundreds of people have helped make this book possible, there are a few in particular I would like to thank: Clay Hebert, David Avrin, Phil Jones, Brad Kolar, Jack Elkins, Steve Bedwell, Mitch Joel, Chris West, Michael Margolis, Greg Satell, Jeffrey Hayzlett, Melissa Agnes, Josh Bernoff, Jenn DeWall, Jesse Finkelstein, Melissa Duffield, Jon Fredrickson, Troy Vom Braucke, Mary Brandon, Braden Kelley, and so many others. Each knowingly—and in some cases unknowingly—contributed to this book. I also would like to thank my Accenture and InnoCentive colleagues, as well as my clients and friends who contributed over the years. It is through these experiences that I gather most of my stories.

The book started life as a pre-release paperback edition titled *25 Lenses*. That version was never formally published, but was printed in limited quantities to get feedback from colleagues. During the pre-release process, I was fortunate to work with Ela Aktay and Kelli Christiansen, both of whom provided great editorial feedback, and Whitney Campbell, who spent countless hours creating the cover.

The book you hold in your hands would never have been completed if it weren't for amazing work of Naren Aryal and his team at

Amplify Publishing. Kristin Perry and Nicole Hall shepherded the book through the entire editorial process—a herculean task! Ricky Frame developed the creative layout, and Danny Moore refined the cover to the final version. Lauren Kanne did an incredible job of editing the manuscript—many times—taking it to a whole new level.

About the Author

As you know, I am a nerd. And proud of it.

My career started after I earned a degree in industrial engineering from Cornell University. My focus was on improving manufacturing productivity. Although I didn't know it at the time, this was the perfect field of study for the work I would eventually do.

Right out of college, I joined Arthur Andersen's Management Information Consulting Division (now Accenture, the global management consulting firm). My first big career opportunity came in 1993, when I helped run our Business Process Reengineering practice. This optimization work was a natural build on my industrial engineering work. Instead of improving manufacturing productivity, we focused on improving business productivity.

After a few years of promoting this work, I experienced an existential crisis when I realized that our process improvement work had led to massive downsizing. During a leave of absence, I evaluated what I wanted to do with my life, and I realized I wanted to help companies grow. And, since 1996, innovation has been my focus.

I was lucky to be given the opportunity to lead a twenty thousand-person process and innovation practice. I gave speeches and workshops to consultants and clients around the world, promoting our perspectives on innovation.

In 2001, I made another shift: I wrote my first book, *24/7 Innovation: A Blueprint for Surviving and Thriving in an Age of Change* (McGraw-Hill), left Accenture, and branched out on my own.

Since then, I've written five books (including the one you're holding). My previous book, *Best Practices Are Stupid: 40 Ways to Out-Innovate the Competition* (Portfolio Penguin) was named the best innovation and creativity book of 2011 by 800-CEO-READ (now, Porchlight Book Company). *Personality Poker*® (Portfolio Penguin), which is both a book and a card game, has been used in thirty-five countries around the world to create high-performing innovation teams.

I have had the great luxury of traveling the world, giving speeches in more than fifty countries. And, in 2015, I was bestowed one of the highest honors of the speaking profession: I was inducted into the Speaker Hall of Fame.

When I'm not speaking on stage, I practice my not-so-sleight-of-hand magic on my family and friends. Amongst my greatest celebrity coups, I had the pleasure of meeting my childhood idol, former *Gong Show* host Chuck Barris. And in 2017, I got to be a judge and mentor on the TLC innovation reality television show, *Girl Starter*.

I now live in Orlando, Florida, where I get to enjoy the most amazing life with my wife.